It's another Quality Book from CGP

This book is for anyone doing GCSE Foundation French.

Whatever subject you're doing it's the same old story — there are lots of facts and you've just got to learn them. KS4 French is no different.

Happily this CGP book gives you all that important information as clearly and concisely as possible.

It's also got some daft bits in to try and make the whole experience at least vaguely entertaining for you.

What CGP is all about

Our sole aim here at CGP is to produce the highest quality books — carefully written, immaculately presented and dangerously close to being funny.

Then we work our socks off to get them out to you — at the cheapest possible prices.

Contents

Section 1 — General Stuff

Section 2 — Lifestyle

Section 3 — Leisure

Section 4 — Holidays

Section 5 — Home and Environment

Section 6 — Education and Work

Section 7 — Grammar

Published by CGP

Contributors:
Angela Billington
Chris Dennett
Lindsay Jordan
Sam Norman
Rachael Powers
Katherine Stewart
Claire Thompson
Jennifer Underwood
Tim Wakeling
James Paul Wallis

With thanks to Sam Norman & Cheryl Robinson
for the proofreading.

No corny clichés about French people were harmed in the making of this book.

ISBN: 978 1 84762 284 6

Groovy website: www.cgpbooks.co.uk
Jolly bits of clipart from CorelDRAW®
Printed by Elanders Ltd, Newcastle upon Tyne.

Based on the classic CGP style created by Richard Parsons.

Numbers

Here we go! Here we go! Here we go! On the count of three — get cracking.

Un, deux, trois — One, two, three...

1. It all starts off easy enough. Learn nought to ten — no problem.

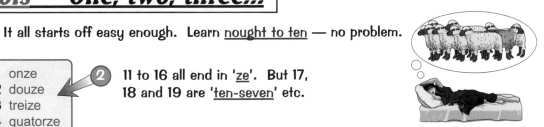

0 zéro
1 un
2 deux
3 trois
4 quatre
5 cinq
6 six
7 sept
8 huit
9 neuf
10 dix

2. 11 to 16 all end in 'ze'. But 17, 18 and 19 are 'ten-seven' etc.

11 onze
12 douze
13 treize
14 quatorze
15 quinze
16 seize
17 dix-sept
18 dix-huit
19 dix-neuf

3. Most 'ten-type' numbers end in 'nte' (except 'vingt') — but 70 is 'sixty-ten' and 80 is 'four-20s'. 90 is 'four-20-ten' — phew!

20	vingt	60	soixante
30	trente	70	soixante-dix
40	quarante	80	quatre-vingts
50	cinquante	90	quatre-vingt-dix

4. The in-between numbers are formed like English — just remember 'et un' for numbers ending in 1. For the 70s and 90s, add the teens to 'soixante' or 'quatre-vingt'.

soixante-treize = seventy-three

Before words which are feminine, like 'fille' or 'voiture', the 'un' or 'et un' changes to 'une' or 'et une'.

21 vingt et un	71 soixante et onze	82 quatre-vingt-deux
22 vingt-deux	72 soixante-douze	95 quatre-vingt-quinze
23 vingt-trois	79 soixante-dix-neuf	98 quatre-vingt-dix-huit

5. When you get to hundreds and thousands, just put cent, deux cent, mille (etc.) before the number.

100	cent
101	cent un
623	six cent vingt-trois
1000	mille
1.000.000	un million

mille neuf cent quarante-sept = 1947

1000 900 40 7

The French put full stops or spaces between digits in long numbers, rather than commas, so ten thousand would be 10.000.

Add -ième to the number to get second, third, etc...

These are easy — just add 'ième' to the number. But '1st' is 'premier' (masc.) or 'première' (fem.).

1st	premier, première	6th	sixième
2nd	deuxième	7th	septième
3rd	troisième	8th	huitième
4th	quatrième	9th	neuvième
5th	cinquième	10th	dixième

1st is written 1er, or 1ère. 2nd is written 2ème, etc.

Watch out for the spellings in blue. And words ending in 'e' (like quatre) lose the 'e' (quatrième).

Prenez la deuxième rue à gauche.

= Take the second street on the left.

Your days are numbered — today's the 10th...

You're bound to know a bit about numbers already — which is cool. And it means you can spend more time checking that you know the rest of the page. Learn all of these words about numbers. The best way to check is to cover up the page and then try to write them down — right now.

Times and Dates

You need to be able to tell the time and understand what time things happen — so if you can't, learn it now.

Quelle heure est-il? — What time is it?

Just as there are loads of ways of saying the time in English, so there are in French too.
Of course, you have to learn all of them.

Quelle heure est-il? = What time is it?

1) Something o'clock:

It's 1 o'clock:	Il est une heure
It's 2 o'clock:	Il est deux heures
It's 8 pm:	Il est vingt heures

2) Quarter to and past, half past:

(It's) quarter past two:	(Il est) deux heures et quart
(It's) half past two:	(Il est) deux heures et demie
(It's) quarter to three:	(Il est) trois heures moins le quart

3) '... past' and '... to':

(It's) twenty past seven:	(Il est) sept heures vingt
(It's) twelve minutes past eight:	(Il est) huit heures douze
(It's) ten to two:	(Il est) deux heures moins dix

4) The 24-hour clock: They use it a lot in France — instead of saying 'a.m. and p.m.'

03:14:	(Il est) trois heures quatorze
20:32:	(Il est) vingt heures trente-deux
19:55:	(Il est) dix-neuf heures cinquante-cinq

C'est quel jour? — What day is it?

More 'vital basics' — they'll earn you simple marks in the exams.

lundi	mardi	mercredi	jeudi	vendredi	samedi	dimanche
					1	2
3	4	5	6	7	8	9
10	11	12	13	14	15	16
17	18	19	20	21	22	23
24	25	26	27	28	29	30

DAYS OF THE WEEK

Monday:	lundi
Tuesday:	mardi
Wednesday:	mercredi
Thursday:	jeudi
Friday:	vendredi
Saturday:	samedi
Sunday:	dimanche

Days of the week are all masculine, with no capital letters. If you want to say 'on Monday', it's 'lundi' — but 'on Mondays' is 'le lundi'.

Je pars mardi.

= I'm going away on Tuesday.

Je fais les courses le mardi.

= I go shopping on Tuesdays (every Tuesday).

SOME USEFUL WORDS ABOUT THE WEEK

today:	aujourd'hui
tomorrow:	demain
yesterday:	hier
the day after tomorrow:	après-demain
the day before yesterday:	avant-hier
week:	la semaine
weekend:	le week-end
on Mondays:	le lundi

He's Caesar? — No, I said, 'Il est six heures'...

Dates and times always come up in the assessments. It's unbelievably important to be able to understand all things clock- and calendar-related. You absolutely have to know the days of the week and things like 'tomorrow' or 'weekend' inside out. So find the time... and get down to it.

Times and Dates

You can bet your bottom dollar you'll find this stuff on dates and times really useful. These essentials will make your sentences sound a whole lot more interesting. It's guaranteed.

Janvier, février, mars, avril...

French months bear a striking resemblance to the English ones — make sure you learn what's different.

Il part en juillet. = He's leaving in July.

Months and seasons are masculine, with no capital letters.

January:	janvier	*July:*	juillet
February:	février	*August:*	août
March:	mars	*September:*	septembre
April:	avril	*October:*	octobre
May:	mai	*November:*	novembre
June:	juin	*December:*	décembre

winter:	hiver
spring:	printemps
summer:	été
autumn:	automne

You say 'au printemps' for in spring. But use 'en' in front of all the other seasons.

You say "the 3 May" instead of "the 3rd of May"

Here's how to say the date in French. This is bound to come up somewhere in your exam — and the examiners won't be impressed if you can't understand what the date is.

Check out p.1 for help with the numbers.

1) In French, they don't say "the third of May" — they say "the three May".

J'arrive le trois octobre. = I am coming on the 3rd of October.

2) The first is the odd one out, because it's more like English. They say "the first May" ("le premier mai").

Ma date de naissance est le premier mars mille neuf cent quatre-vingt-treize.

= My date of birth is the first of March 1993.

3) And this is how you write the date in a letter:

Londres, le 5 mars 2009

= London, 5th March 2009

See p.10-11 for letters.

4) And here are some other useful bits:

in the year 2000:	en l'an deux mille
in 2009:	en deux mille neuf

NOT 'deux mille et neuf'

Ce matin — This morning... Ce soir — This evening

You'll use these phrases all the time — they're great for making loads of arrangements.

Je fais souvent du ski. = I often go skiing.

always:	toujours
sometimes:	quelquefois
(quite) often:	(assez) souvent
(quite) rarely:	(assez) rarement

See p.100 for how to say you never do something.

this morning:	ce matin
this afternoon:	cet après-midi
this evening/tonight:	ce soir
tomorrow morning:	demain matin
this week:	cette semaine
next week:	la semaine prochaine
last week:	la semaine dernière
this weekend:	ce week-end

Qu'est-ce que tu fais ce soir ? = What are you doing tonight?

Dates — better at the cinema than in French...

It doesn't come much more crucial than this. It will get you more marks — the examiners specifically say that they want you to know this stuff. It's not that hard, either. You have to learn the phrase 'Qu'est-ce que tu fais ce soir?', and the words you can slot in instead of 'ce soir'.

Asking Questions

Curiosity may have killed the cat, but you've got to be able to understand and ask questions — so learn this.

Quand — When... Pourquoi — Why... Où — Where

when?	quand?
why?	pourquoi?
where?	où?
how?	comment?
how much/many?	combien de...?
at what time...?	à quelle heure...?
who/whom?	qui?
which...?	quel(le)...?

Learn these question words — they're pretty important.

Quand est-ce que tu rentres? = When are you coming back?

Qui a cassé la fenêtre? = Who broke the window?

Quelle est la date? = What is the date?

'Quel' is a tricky question word. It has different meanings in English and has to agree with the object it's talking about. It has masc., fem., singular and plural forms.

which...? what...?:	
quel...?	quels...?
quelle...?	quelles...?

Quels vêtements allez-vous porter? = Which clothes are you going to wear?

1) Use Est-ce que to start questions

To turn a statement into a yes-no question, put 'Est-ce que' onto the beginning of the sentence.

See p.80 for why there's an 's' here.

Est-ce que tes bananes sont jaunes? = Are your bananas yellow?

To answer yes to a question containing a negative, use 'si'.

Est-ce que tu n'as pas soif? = Aren't you thirsty?

Si, j'ai soif. = Yes, I'm thirsty.

If your question starts with 'What...', use 'Qu'est-ce que'.

Qu'est-ce que tu manges le soir? = What do you eat in the evening?

OR... *Que manges-tu le soir?*

You can start the question with 'Que' — but the verb (manges) and the subject (tu) switch places in the question and a hyphen (-) is added.

2) Ask a question by putting the verb first

In English, you change 'I can go' to 'Can I go?' to make it a question. It's exactly the same in French except you need to add a hyphen (-) between the subject and the verb.

Est-elle partie? = Has she gone?

Veux-tu m'aider? = Do you want to help me?

3) Ask a question by changing your tone of voice

The third way to ask questions is easy — say a normal sentence but raise your voice at the end...

Tu as des frères ou des sœurs? = Do you have any brothers or sisters? (Literally: You have brothers or sisters?)

If you have a question for her, why not 'est-ce que'...

This page is full of question words — start by learning them all. Shut the book and write down all the question words at the top of the page. Look back for the ones you missed and try again till you get them all. Then, all you need to do is remember the three main ways to ask a question.

Being Polite

OK, you may know all of the French covered so far, but it won't look good if the first thing you say to an actual French speaker is "Hello Bogface" — try opening with these superb gems of politeness instead.

Bonjour — Hello

Learn these phrases — they're crucial. Nuff said.

Bonjour:	Hello
Salut:	Hi
Bienvenue:	Welcome
Bonsoir:	Good evening
Bonne nuit:	Good night
Au revoir:	Goodbye

Bon anniversaire:	Happy birthday
Bon week-end:	Have a good weekend
Bonne chance:	Good luck

Comment ça va? — How are you?

Keeping a conversation going is easy if you use a few of these lil' sparklers.

Comment ça va? = How are you?

Et toi? = And you? (Informal)

Comment allez vous? = How are you? (Polite)

Et vous? = And you? (Polite)

'Tu' and 'vous' both mean 'you' in French. If you're talking to someone older than you, or to a stranger, you usually use 'vous'. Only if you're talking to friends, family or other young people should you use 'tu'.

Ça va bien, merci. = I am fine, thanks.

You can just say 'Bien, merci' (you might get more marks for the whole thing, though).

See p.22 if you're not well and you need to explain why.

Other possible answers

Not good:	Ça ne va pas bien.
Not bad:	Pas mal.
Great!:	Super!
I feel awful:	Je me sens affreux / affreuse.
OK:	Comme ci comme ça.

Voici Matthew — This is Matthew

Other useful stuff you should know...

Enchanté(e). = Pleased to meet you. (Literally 'enchanted')

Entre. Assieds-toi. = Come in. Sit down. (Familiar, singular)

Entrez. Asseyez-vous. = Come in. Sit down. (Formal or plural)

Merci bien. C'est très gentil. = Thank you. That's very kind.

Awfully sorry, but I don't know how to be polite...

It's a bit boring, I know. But grin, bear it, and most of all learn it, and you'll be fine. It'll be worth it when you've passed your GCSE with flying colours — this is guaranteed to improve your marks.

Being Polite

You'll be expected to use appropriate language in your assessments, so if I can't get away with saying, 'Oh just get on and learn this, hairy-toes', then you can't get away with rude-isms either.

Je voudrais — I would like

It's more polite to say 'je voudrais' (I would like) than 'je veux' (I want).

Here's how to say you would like a thing:

Je voudrais du pain. = I would like some bread.

Here's how to say you would like to do something:

Je voudrais voyager en Europe. = I would like to travel in Europe.

She would like: Elle voudrait

See p.4 for other ways to ask questions, p.103 for more info on the conditional, and p.14-15 for help on asking for things at the dinner table.

S'il vous plaît — Please... Merci — Thank you

Easy stuff — maybe the first French words you ever learnt. Don't forget them.

s'il vous plaît = please (formal)

This is for when you're calling the person 'vous'. If you call them 'tu', you need to say: 's'il te plaît'. See p.5.

merci = thank you

You're welcome: De rien

Je suis désolé(e) — I'm sorry

Here are a couple of ways to apologise — learn them both, and how they're used.

Je suis désolé(e). = I'm sorry.

Add an 'e' here if you're female.

Pardon. = I'm sorry.

Use this one if you're talking to a friend or someone you know well.

Est-ce que je peux...? — May I...?

Excusez-moi... = Excuse me... (Polite)

You can use this if you want to ask someone the way.

...est-ce que je peux m'asseoir ? = ...may I sit down?

go to the toilet: aller aux toilettes

Merci? — you'll get none of that from us...

These little beauties are just the ticket for charming your way around France... absolutely vital. A really common mistake with this stuff is to say 's'il vous plaît' to someone who you're calling 'tu'. Tsk. That kind of thing is really important to get right in your speaking and writing assessments.

Opinions

It pays to have an opinion. Learn how to say what you think... in many different ways. Genius.

Say what you think — it'll sound impressive...

You'll often be asked what you think of stuff. So get learning these handy phrases.

Sport? It's great. Just great.

J'aime le tennis de table, mais je n'aime pas le football.

= I like table tennis, but I don't like football.

LIKING THINGS

I like...	J'aime...
I like...	...me plaît
I'm interested in...	Je m'intéresse à...
I find ... great	Je trouve ... chouette
I like ... a lot	J'aime bien...

DISLIKING THINGS

I don't like...	Je n'aime pas...
I don't like...	...ne me plaît pas
...doesn't interest me	...ne m'intéresse pas
I find ... awful	Je trouve ... affreux/affreuse

J'aime bien le football, mais je préfère le basket.

= I like football a lot, but I prefer basketball.

OTHER USEFUL PHRASES

It's all right:	Ça va
I don't mind / care:	Ça m'est égal
I prefer...	Je préfère...

Watch out — 'J'aime Pierre' means 'I love Pierre'. To say you like him, try 'Je trouve Pierre sympa' *(I think Pierre's nice).*

See p.100 for more on how to say what you don't like and don't do.

Qu'est-ce que tu penses de...? — What do you think of...?

All these nifty phrases mean pretty much the same thing — 'What do you think of ...?'. If you can use all of them, your French will be more interesting — and that means more marks.

FINDING OUT SOMEONE'S OPINION

What do you think of...?:	Qu'est-ce que tu penses de...?
What's your opinion of...?:	Quel est ton avis de...?
What do you think?:	Qu'est-ce que tu penses?
How do you find...?:	Comment trouves-tu...?
Do you find him/her nice?:	Est-ce que tu le/la trouves sympa?

I THINK...

I think that... :	Je pense que...
I think that... :	Je crois que...
I think ... is ... :	Je trouve ... ...

Qu'est-ce que tu penses de mon petit ami?

= What do you think of my boyfriend?

Je pense qu'il est affreux.

= I think that he's awful.

Comment dit-on 'dunno' en français...

Never underestimate the power of opinions. It might seem hard to believe, but they really do want you to say what you think. Make sure you learn one way to say 'I like' and 'I don't like' first. They're the absolute basics — you'll get nowhere without them. Then cram in all the fancy bits.

Opinions

Don't just say that you like or hate something — really blow your teacher away by explaining why. Go for it — and knock their socks clean off.

Use these words to describe things

Describing words are adjectives. See p.80-82 for more on this.

Here's a whole load of words to describe things you like or don't like. They're dead easy to use, so it really is worth learning them.

good:	bon(ne)	*fantastic:*	formidable / fantastique	*marvellous:*	merveilleux / merveilleuse
great:	chouette	*interesting:*	intéressant(e)	*bad:*	mauvais(e)
beautiful:	beau / belle	*brilliant:*	génial(e)	*awful:*	affreux / affreuse
friendly:	amical(e)	*nice (person):*	sympa	*nice / kind:*	gentil(le)
splendid:	magnifique				

Bob est super.

= Bob is great.

Les filles sont affreuses.

= The girls are awful.

For 'because' say 'parce que'

To make your opinion more convincing, give a reason for it. The best way to do that is to use the handy phrase 'parce que' — 'because'.

J'aime bien ce film, parce que les acteurs sont formidables.

= I like this film a lot, because the actors are fantastic.

Je trouve ce film affreux, parce que l'histoire est ennuyeuse.

= I think this film is awful, because the story is boring.

J'adore jouer du violon, parce que je trouve la musique classique très belle.

= I love playing the violin, because I find classical music very beautiful.

If you hear the word 'car', it means 'because'

It's handy to know that 'car', like 'parce que', means 'because'. Nothing to do with cars at all.

Elle est très fatiguée, car elle travaille tout le temps.

= She is very tired, because she works all the time.

Because, because, because, because, because...

It's not much cop only knowing how to ask someone else's opinion, or how to say 'I think', without being able to say what and why you think. All these phrases are easy — just stick them together to get a sentence. Just make sure you don't say something daft like 'I hate it because it's lovely'.

What Do You Think of...?

If you want a good grade, your teacher needs to hear your opinions.

Use 'je trouve...' to give your opinion

Giving opinions is really important in French. It shows that you can be creative with the language.

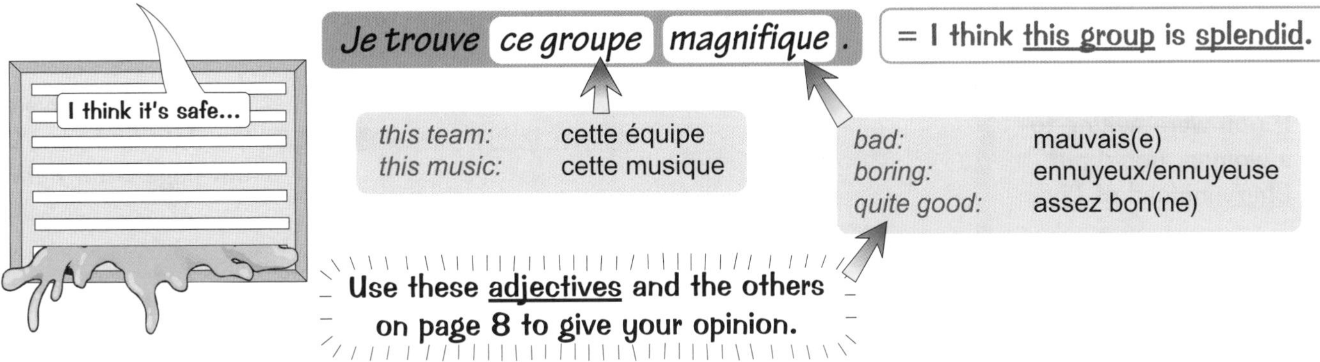

I think it's safe...
Je trouve ce groupe magnifique.
= I think this group is splendid.
this team: cette équipe
this music: cette musique
bad: mauvais(e)
boring: ennuyeux/ennuyeuse
quite good: assez bon(ne)
Use these adjectives and the others on page 8 to give your opinion.

Est-ce que tu aimes...? — Do you like...?

You'll also need to be able to understand the opinions of others.

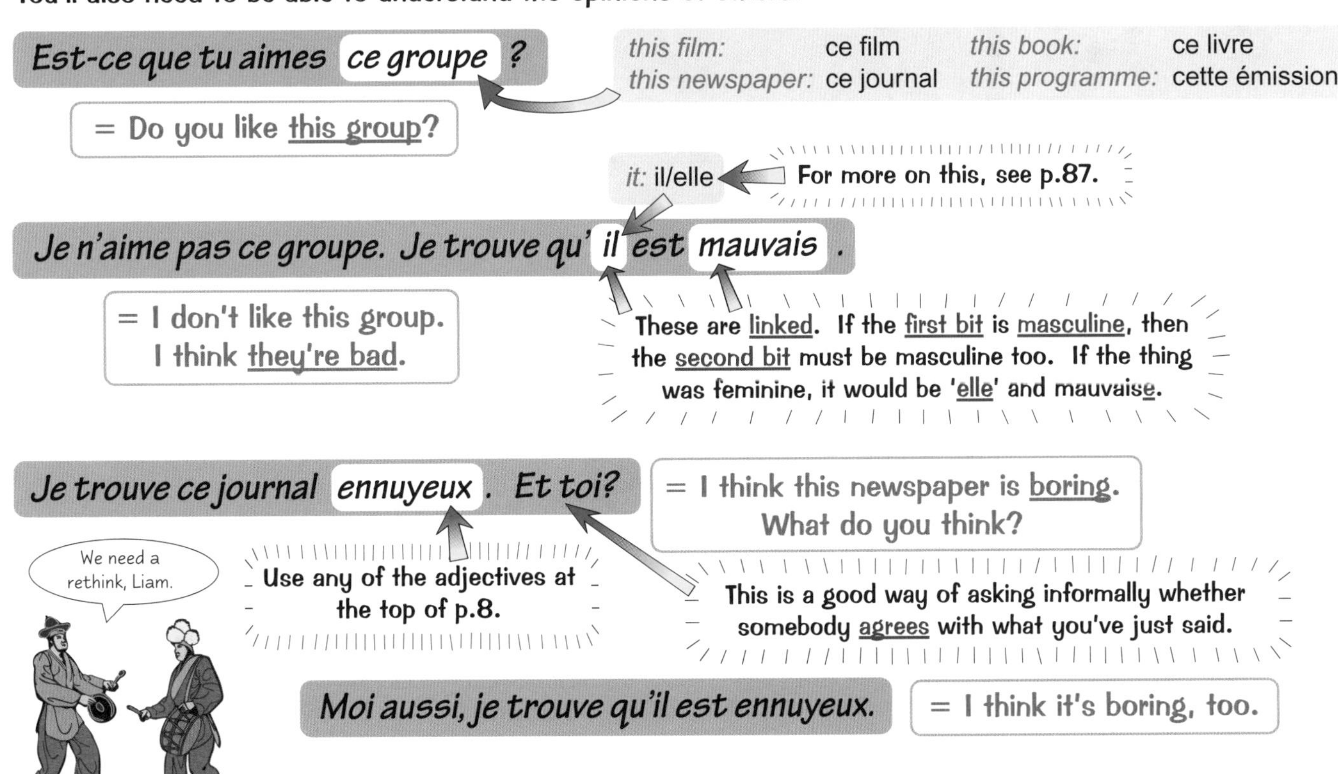

Est-ce que tu aimes ce groupe?
= Do you like this group?
this film: ce film
this newspaper: ce journal
this book: ce livre
this programme: cette émission
it: il/elle
For more on this, see p.87.
Je n'aime pas ce groupe. Je trouve qu'il est mauvais.
= I don't like this group. I think they're bad.
These are linked. If the first bit is masculine, then the second bit must be masculine too. If the thing was feminine, it would be 'elle' and mauvaise.
Je trouve ce journal ennuyeux. Et toi?
= I think this newspaper is boring. What do you think?
Use any of the adjectives at the top of p.8.
This is a good way of asking informally whether somebody agrees with what you've just said.
We need a rethink, Liam.
Moi aussi, je trouve qu'il est ennuyeux.
= I think it's boring, too.

Useful stuff, in my opinion...

Giving your opinion about things gets you big marks in the assessments. It's quite easy to say why you like something, so you've got no excuses — you've just got to learn these phrases.

Writing Informal Letters

I just know you're gonna be chuffed to bits when I tell you that you're bound to have to write a letter in French at some point — it could very easily be in your written assessment.

Start a letter with 'Cher Bob' — 'Dear Bob'

Learn the layout of letters, and how to say 'Dear Blank...' and all that stuff. It's essential. This letter's short on content, but it shows you how to start and end it properly, and where to put the date.

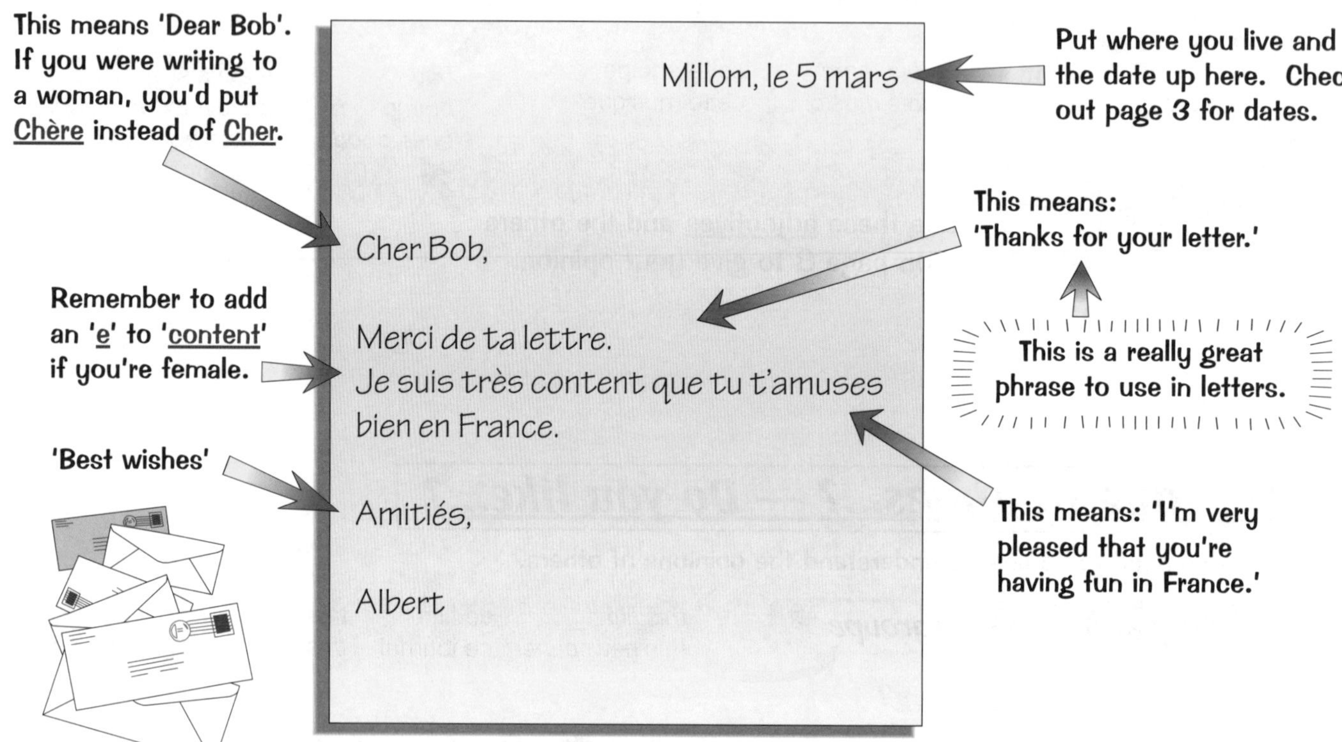

This means 'Dear Bob'. If you were writing to a woman, you'd put Chère instead of Cher.
Millom, le 5 mars
Put where you live and the date up here. Check out page 3 for dates.
Cher Bob,
This means: 'Thanks for your letter.'
Remember to add an 'e' to 'content' if you're female.
Merci de ta lettre.
Je suis très content que tu t'amuses bien en France.
This is a really great phrase to use in letters.
'Best wishes'
Amitiés,
Albert
This means: 'I'm very pleased that you're having fun in France.'

Use these phrases in your letters

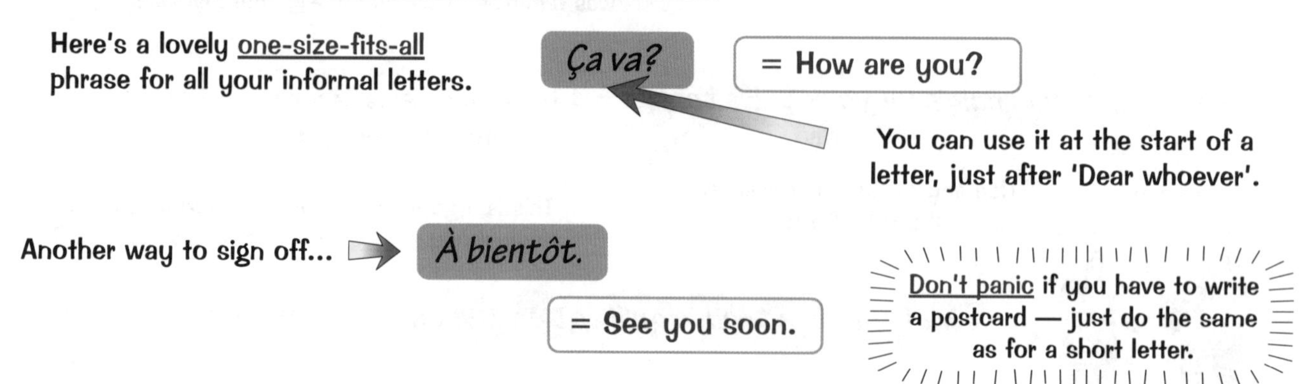

French letters — let's keep it clean...

For once, some fairly easy stuff — hurrah. It's the bread and butter of your written work. Make sure you know the French stock phrases really well — then your letter will sound dead smart and authentic. Just write the main part like you would write to a friend in English. In French, obviously.

Writing Formal Letters

You may be asked to write a formal letter as well — it's a bit mean, but sadly you've no choice. On the plus side, you might have to write a letter of complaint — everyone likes complaining... Study the basic format below and practise creating some formal letters of your own.

Put your name and address at the top left

Letters — they really are just as simple as this...

It looks impressive if you put your name and address at the top. (In French, the addresses go the opposite way round to in English — sender on the left, recipient on the right.)

The name and address of who you're writing to goes here.

Aleesha Thompson
16 Rusland Drive
Manchester
M14 7ZN
Grande-Bretagne

Hôtel Saint Michel
16, rue des Papillons
Paris
France

le 20 avril 2010

Put the date here.

Put this if you don't know the person's name or gender. If you know it's Monsieur Claude Terrier, put that above his address and write 'Monsieur' here.

Monsieur / Madame,

J'ai passé deux nuits à l'Hôtel Saint Michel entre le 12 et le 14 avril. Les employés étaient super et très agréables et la chambre était propre.

Malheureusement, je ne suis pas du tout contente de mon séjour parce que la douche n'a pas marché, la télévision était cassée et il y avait trop de bruit partout, donc je n'ai pas très bien dormi.

Veuillez agréer, Monsieur/Madame, l'expression de mes sentiments distingués.

A. Thompson

Aleesha Thompson

This little lot simply means: I spent two nights at the Saint Michel Hotel between the 12th and the 14th of April. The employees were great and very kind and the room was clean.

Unfortunately, I'm not at all happy with my stay because the shower didn't work, the TV was broken and there was too much noise everywhere, so I didn't sleep very well.

All this just means 'Yours sincerely'. (See below)

Check out page 49 for problems vocab and page 75 for help writing a job application letter.

Learn these ways to end a letter

This set ending is quite long, I'm afraid — just learn it and churn it out.

Je vous prie d'agréer, Monsieur ,
l'expression de mes sentiments distingués.

to a woman: Madame

= Yours faithfully / sincerely

Another useful phrase: *Je vous remercie d'avance.* = Many thanks in advance.

How to end a letter — just stop writing...

I know, I know — letter structure needs a lot of effort to get it firmly lodged in your brain. And then there are set polite phrases for formal French letters just like there are in English — it's essential that you know the right ones for the start and end. Get scribbling some practice letters.

Revision Summary

This section includes all the absolute basics... with a few lessons in letter writing thrown in for good measure. All the bits on your opinions, and on dates and times (including today, tomorrow, every week, on Mondays etc.) can make a huge difference to your marks. Go back over the section again until you can answer every one of the questions here first time — without hesitation.

1) Count out loud from 1 to 20 in French.
2) How do you say these numbers in French? a) 22 b) 35 c) 58 d) 71 e) 112
3) What are these in French? a) 1st b) 4th c) 7th d) 19th
4) Ask 'What time is it?' in French.
How would you say these times in French? a) 5:00 b) 10:30 c) 13:22 d) 16:45
5) Say all the days of the week in French, from Monday to Sunday.
6) How do you say these in French? a) yesterday b) today c) tomorrow
7) Say all of the months of the year in French, from January to December.
8) How do you say the date of your birthday in French?
9) 'Qu'est-ce que tu fais ce soir?' means 'What are you doing this evening?'
How would you say, 'What are you doing: a) this afternoon?' b) this morning?' c) next week?'
10) 'Tu chantes' means 'You sing' or 'You are singing'. What do these questions mean?
a) Pourquoi tu chantes? b) Où est-ce que tu chantes? c) Qu'est-ce que tu chantes?
d) Chantes-tu bien? e) Quand est-ce que tu chantes? f) Est-ce que tu chantes?
11) What's the French for? a) Please b) Thank you c) How are you? d) I'm sorry
12) How would you ask someone what they think of Elvis Presley? (In French.)
13) How would you say these things in French? Give at least one way to say each of them.
a) I like Elvis Presley. b) I don't like Elvis Presley. c) I find Elvis Presley interesting.
d) I find Elvis Presley awful. e) I think that Elvis Presley is fantastic.
14) To win this week's star prize, complete the following sentence in 10 words or fewer (in French): 'J'aime Elvis Presley parce que...'
15) You like the group 'The Sheep Shearers', but you think 'James and the Infinite Monkeys' are brilliant. How would you tell someone that in French? (Leave the band names in English.)
16) Write a letter to your friend Marie-Claire. Write your address, say hello and say you hope she's having fun in France. You want to put 'see you soon' at the end — how would you do that?
17) Which side of the page does your address go on in a formal French letter?
18) How would you end a formal letter in French?
19) What does this phrase mean: 'Je vous remercie d'avance'? Is it for a formal or informal letter?

Food

You need to learn the vocab for all the basic food, especially the things you like and eat often. There's a lot of information to digest here, but the more you know, the better.

L'épicerie et la boucherie — Greengrocer's and Butcher's

This is basic, meat and two veg vocab. You really do need to know it.

VEGETABLES: les légumes (masc.)

potato:	la pomme de terre
carrot:	la carotte
tomato:	la tomate
cauliflower:	le chou-fleur
French beans:	les haricots verts
lettuce:	la salade
mushroom:	le champignon
cabbage:	le chou
peas:	les petits pois

MEAT and FISH: la viande et le poisson

pork:	le porc	*beef:*	le bœuf
sausage:	la saucisse	*steak:*	le bifteck
salami:	le saucisson	*chicken:*	le poulet
ham:	le jambon	*seafood:*	les fruits de mer (masc.)

Les boissons et les desserts — Drinks and Desserts

Every decent meal needs a dessert and a drink.

DRINKS: les boissons (fem.)

tea:	le thé
coffee:	le café
beer:	la bière
cider:	le cidre
wine:	le vin
coke:	le coca
fruit juice:	le jus de fruit
lemonade:	la limonade
mineral water:	l'eau minérale (fem.)

DESSERTS: les desserts (masc.)

cake:	le gâteau
biscuit:	le biscuit
ice cream:	la glace
pancake:	la crêpe
yogurt:	le yaourt
jam:	la confiture
chocolate:	le chocolat
sweets:	les bonbons (masc.)

FRUITS: les fruits (masc.)

apple:	la pomme
banana:	la banane
strawberry:	la fraise
raspberry:	la framboise
cherry:	la cerise
apricot:	l'abricot (masc.)
peach:	la pêche
pear:	la poire
lemon:	le citron

D'autres choses à manger — Other things to eat

Here are some more basic foods — learn them really well.

OTHER THINGS TO EAT: d'autres choses à manger

bread:	le pain	*sugar:*	le sucre	*soup:*	la soupe
milk:	le lait	*salt:*	le sel	*pasta:*	les pâtes (fem.)
cream:	la crème	*pepper:*	le poivre	*cereals:*	les céréales (fem.)
butter:	le beurre	*rice:*	le riz	*chips:*	les frites (fem.)
cheese:	le fromage	*egg:*	l'œuf (masc.)	*crisps:*	les chips (fem.)

Learn the crêpe out of this page...

A lot of foods are easy to remember in French — like le biscuit, la crème, le café... But some aren't — you just have to learn the tricky ones. Food's dead important to French people — it's almost certain to be mentioned in the exams somewhere, so all this stuff is well worth knowin'...

Mealtimes

You can use the vocab on this page to be polite in French, at any time, in any situation, if politeness is what's required — when you meet Monsieur le Président, for example.

Voudriez-vous...? — Would you like...?

'Voudriez' is in the conditional — see p. 103.

This is another form of that useful verb 'vouloir'.

Voudriez-vous ***le sel*** *?* = Would you like the salt?

the pepper: le poivre — the wine: le vin — the butter: le beurre

Est-ce que je peux vous passer ***une serviette*** *?* = Can I pass you a napkin?

Voudriez-vous ***manger*** *?* = Would you like to eat?

to drink: boire

Oui, je veux bien. = Yes please.

Non, merci. = No thanks.

Either 'Oui, je veux bien' or 'Oui, merci' sound more French than 'Oui, s'il vous plaît'.

Est-ce que tu as faim ou soif? — Are you hungry or thirsty?

Questions like these are important. Make sure you understand them, or you may go hungry... or lose marks.

Est-ce que tu as ***faim*** *?* = Are you hungry?

thirsty: soif

J'ai ***faim*** *.* = I'm hungry.

thirsty: soif

Non, merci. Je n'ai pas ***faim*** *.* = No thanks. I'm not hungry.

Est-ce que je peux...? — May I...?

Use this nifty phrase properly and you'll be the soul of politeness.

Est-ce que je peux avoir ***le sel*** *, s'il vous plaît?* = May I have the salt, please?

a napkin: une serviette — the sugar: le sucre

You'd like the salt? Just help your sel...

Make sure you remain polite in French at all times... You never know who might be listening... But politeness is the key to showing you've mastered the language and it's the ticket to passing that GCSE. So throw in some lovely conditionals where you can and you'll be laughing. Politely.

Mealtimes

This stuff is really useful. And it fits tons of different situations too. Bonus.

Je ne mange pas de... — I don't eat...

Je suis désolé(e). Je ne mange pas de petits pois. = I'm sorry. I don't eat peas.

meat: viande (fem.)

See p.13 for more foods.

always: toujours

Je mange souvent des fruits. J'adore les fruits. = I often eat fruit. I love fruit.

Je suis végétarien(ne). = I'm a vegetarian.

Tu manges en famille? — Do you eat with your family?

This bit shows that you can link the family and food topics.

See p.18 for more family members.

On mange toujours en famille. = We always eat as a family.

alone: seul(e)

Mon père travaille tard, donc on ne mange pas ensemble. = My dad works late, so we don't eat together.

My mother:	Ma mère
My sister:	Ma sœur
My brother:	Mon frère

goes swimming:	fait de la natation
plays football:	joue au foot
goes ice skating:	va à la patinoire

If you only want a little, ask for 'un peu'

These amount words are dead useful.

a bit: un peu

Je voudrais beaucoup de sucre, s'il vous plaît. = I would like lots of sugar, please.

Je voudrais un grand morceau de gâteau. = I would like a big piece of cake.

J'ai assez mangé, merci. = I've eaten enough, thanks.

a lot: beaucoup *trop:* too much

Ça suffit. = That's enough.

For more quantities, look at page 34.

Est-ce que ça vous a plu? — Did you like it?

You'd get asked this question in most restaurants and it might pop up in your listening exam.

Le repas était bon. = The meal was good.

very good:	très bon
bad:	mauvais
very bad:	très mauvais
delicious:	délicieux

Le repas n'était pas bon. = The meal wasn't good.

Que c'est bon, que c'est bon...

I for one seriously love French food. They're really big on high-quality, fresh produce. You can see that just by going round a French market. The fruit stalls look like a beautiful Renoir painting.

Daily Routine

Chores and revision — two peas from the same pod. But unlike ironing, once done, revision is done for ever.

Parle-moi de ta journée — Tell me about your day

Daily routine. Learn it. Work it. Know it like it's... um... routine.

Je me réveille à sept heures. = I wake up at seven o'clock.

I get up:	Je me lève	*I go to bed:*	Je me couche
I go to school:	Je vais au collège	*I work:*	Je travaille

See page 2 for more info about time.

Est-ce que tu fais le ménage? — Do you do the housework?

Even if you never help at home, learn these words.

Je fais la vaisselle à la maison. = I wash up at home.

I do the laundry:	Je fais la lessive
I do the shopping:	Je fais les courses
I wash the car:	Je lave la voiture
I do the gardening:	Je fais le jardinage
I walk the dog:	Je promène le chien

Je dois faire la vaisselle. = I have to wash up.

do the laundry:	faire la lessive
do the shopping:	faire les courses
wash the car:	laver la voiture
do the gardening:	faire le jardinage
walk the dog:	promener le chien

Je gagne de l'argent de poche pour aider à la maison. = I earn pocket money for helping at home.

These verbs are all in the infinitive (see page 91).

As-tu besoin de quelque chose? — Do you need anything?

In your listening exam, you might hear someone asking for something or offering to help out...

Est-ce que vous avez du savon? = Do you have any soap?

a towel: une serviette *an aspirin:* une aspirine

Est-ce que je peux prendre une douche? = May I take a shower?

have a towel: avoir une serviette

Est-ce que je peux vous aider? = Can I help you?

Est-ce que je peux faire la vaisselle? = Can I wash up?

lay the table: mettre la table *do the washing:* faire la lessive

Your turn to do the housework — ménage à toi...

OK, it might not be the most exciting way to spend your youthful years, but it's not really hard. It's just about sitting down and learning the words. Commit them to memory and you're away.

About Yourself

You might already know some of this stuff, but it's ultra-important, so make sure you know it back to front. Talking about yourself in your speaking or writing assessment — it's pretty much a dead cert.

Parle-moi de toi-même — Tell me about yourself

These are the basics. Learn them all.

What are you called?: Comment tu t'appelles?

Je m'appelle Angela. = I'm called Angela.

How old are you?: Quel âge as-tu?

J'ai quinze ans. = I'm 15 years old.

When is your birthday?: Quand est ton anniversaire?

Mon anniversaire est le douze décembre. = My birthday is the 12th of December.

See pages 60-61 for where you live, page 1 for more numbers and page 3 for more dates.

Where do you live?: Où habites-tu?

J'habite à Lancaster. = I live in Lancaster.

What do you like?: Qu'est-ce que tu aimes?

J'aime le football. = I like football.

You can use this to say you like anything, but be careful: 'Je t'aime' means 'I love you'.

Comment es-tu? — What are you like?

You have to describe how gorgeous you are as well — you can lie in writing, but not when speaking.

Je suis grand(e). = I am tall.

short: petit(e)
fat: gros(se)
thin: maigre
slim: mince

medium height: de taille moyenne

For more colours, see page 35.

J'ai les yeux marron. = I have brown eyes.

blue: bleus
green: verts

'Marron' is a strange adjective — it doesn't need an 's' on the end even though 'yeux' is plural.

long: noirs *short:* courts

J'ai les cheveux blonds. = I have blonde hair.

black: noirs *brown:* bruns *red:* roux *dark:* foncés *light:* clairs

England
Dear Simon,
I am a sixteen-year-old-girl with blackish hair, fair skin and brown eyes.

Comment ça s'écrit? — How do you spell that?

You may have to spell your name and home town letter by letter in your speaking assessments. Here's how to pronounce the letters of the French alphabet. Practise going through it out loud — yes, you'll sound daft, but you'd sound dafter getting it wrong in the assessments.

A — ah (like in 'car')
B — bay
C — say
D — day
E — eu (like in 'peu')
F — eff
G — jay ('j' like 'g' in 'beige')
H — ash
I — ee (like in 'me')
J — jee ('j' like 'g' in 'beige')
K — kah
L — ell
M — em
N — en
O — oh
P — pay
Q — kue ('ue' like in 'tu')
R — air
S — ess
T — tay
U — ue (as in 'tu')
V — vay
W — doob le vay
X — eex
Y — ee-grek
Z — zed

é — aigu
è — grave
ê — circonflexe

For letters with accents, you just say the letter followed by the accent, so 'â' would be 'ah circonflexe'.

I'm tall, handsome, witty, a compulsive liar...

Learn how to ask and answer questions about yourself, and make darn sure you know the French alphabet. It's the kind of thing that could crop up in the listening exam — e.g. there'll be someone saying they're from a random French town you won't have heard of, and then they'll spell it out.

Family and Pets

You might have to talk or write about your family situation and your pets — it's best to be prepared...

J'ai une sœur — I have one sister

The average family

To describe your family structure, use these sentences:

J'ai deux frères et une sœur. = I have two brothers and one sister.

Ils s'appellent Jack, Henry et Charlotte. = They are called Jack, Henry and Charlotte.

'Ils' is used for a group of males or a mixture of males and females.

a girlfriend: une petite amie

J'ai un petit ami. = I have a boyfriend.

boyfriend: petit ami

Je n'ai pas de petite amie. = I don't have a girlfriend.

Ma sœur / Mon frère est... — My sister / brother is...

Remember, detail is key in the assessments. Use these phrases to describe your family in more detail:

Il a douze ans. = He's 12 years old.

Elle a les yeux bleus. = She has blue eyes.

My father:	Mon père	*My stepmother:*	Ma belle-mère	*My girlfriend:*	Ma petite amie/ma copine
My brother:	Mon frère	*My stepfather:*	Mon beau-père	*My boyfriend:*	Mon petit ami/mon copain
My sister:	Ma sœur	*My grandmother:*	Ma grand-mère		
My mother:	Ma mère	*My grandfather:*	Mon grand-père		
My aunt:	Ma tante	*My wife:*	Ma femme		
My uncle:	Mon oncle	*My husband:*	Mon mari		

Il est marié. = He's married.

separated: séparé(e) *divorced:* divorcé(e)

Est-ce que tu as des animaux domestiques? — Have you any pets?

a cat:	un chat	*a guinea pig:*	un cochon d'Inde
a bird:	un oiseau	*a rabbit:*	un lapin
a fish:	un poisson	*a mouse:*	une souris
a horse:	un cheval	*a hamster:*	un hamster

Animals. Always useful vocab to know. And oh so cute...

Non, je n'ai pas d'animaux. = No, I don't have any animals.

Oui, j'ai un chien. = Yes, I have a dog.

Mon chien s'appelle Cannelle. = My dog is called Cannelle.

Il est marron. = He is brown.

Swap in any descriptive word here.

See page 35 for colours, page 17 for things like fat and thin, and page 100 for more info on negatives.

No pets — just make something up...

This stuff is pretty straightforward. You learn the sentence, learn the words, and just slot in whichever words you need. There's no excuse for not being able to do this stuff — learn it.

Personality

It helps you connect to other people, makes or breaks that job interview, could win you a spot on X Factor or in the hearts of the nation, and it's who you are. It's personality, and it's important.

Comment es-tu? — What are you like?

You might be asked to talk about your personality in the speaking tasks, so here goes...

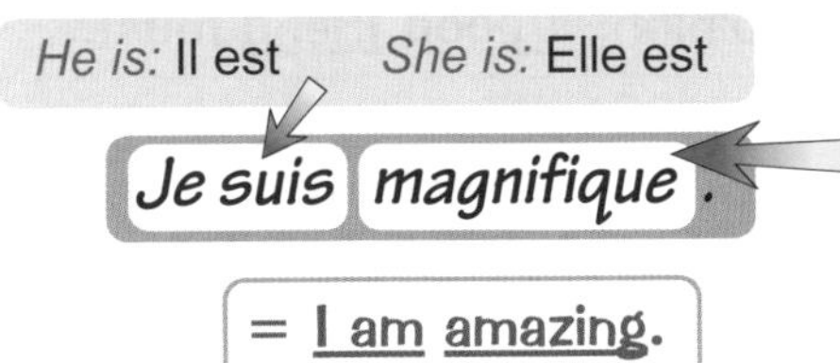

He is: Il est
She is: Elle est
Je suis magnifique.
= I am amazing.

nice:	agréable / sympa	*friendly:*	amical(e)
funny:	amusant(e) / drôle	*kind:*	aimable / gentil(le)
lively:	plein(e) de vie / animé(e)	*hard-working:*	travailleur / travailleuse
chatty:	bavard(e)		

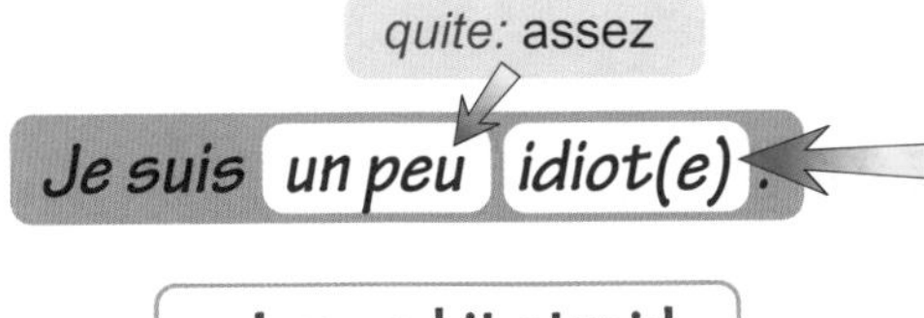

quite: assez
Je suis un peu idiot(e).
= I am a bit stupid.

impatient:	impatient(e)	*selfish:*	égoïste
mean:	méchant(e)	*shy:*	timide
boring:	ennuyeux / ennuyeuse	*sad:*	triste
lazy:	paresseux / paresseuse		

bad: mauvais

J'ai un bon sens de l'humour. = I have a good sense of humour.

Oh we do, do we? Go on then, amuse us...

La personalité des autres — Other people's personalities

Talking about other people's personalities is simple — just use these celeb examples as guidelines...

Je respecte beaucoup Reese Witherspoon. = I respect Reese Witherspoon a lot.

Elle est travailleuse, optimiste et pleine de vie. = She's hard-working, optimistic and full of life.

You can put any of the personality traits above in these white boxes.

Elle est aussi une bonne mère. = She's also a good mother.

Lewis Hamilton est travailleur, bavard et gentil. = Lewis Hamilton is hard-working, chatty and kind.

You need to use the right form of the adjective — e.g it's "travailleur" for a man, and "travailleuse" for a woman.

Am I decisive? Well, yes and no...

This personality vocab isn't just useful for GCSE French — it could also come in handy to describe the man or woman of your dreams if you're ever a contestant on Blind Date in France...

Relationships and Future Plans

This page is particularly useful if you want to send a letter to a French agony aunt.

Un bon ami doit être... — A good friend must be...

It's good to know the qualities you're looking for...

an ideal partner: un(e) partenaire idéal(e)

À mon avis, un(e) bon(ne) ami(e) doit ... = In my opinion, a good friend must...

be kind:	être gentil(le)	*be chatty:*	être bavard(e)
be fun:	être amusant(e)	*be there for me:*	être là pour moi
be nice:	être sympa	*be like me:*	être comme moi

On s'entend bien ensemble... — We get on well together...

Sometimes relationships are plain sailing...

Je m'entends bien avec mon ami(e). = I get on well with my friend.

Nous sommes meilleur(e)s ami(e)s. = We are best friends.

my mother: ma mère *my sister:* ma sœur *my brother:* mon frère

Il me plaît. = I fancy him.

...and sometimes they're not...

On ne se comprend pas. = We don't understand each other.

Elle est trop égoïste. = She's too selfish.

On se dispute toujours. = We argue all the time.

Il ne m'écoute pas. = He doesn't listen to me.

She doesn't listen to me: Elle ne m'écoute pas
They don't listen to me: Ils ne m'écoutent pas

Je voudrais me marier... — I'd like to get married...

It's good to have a plan. If you're not sure of your relationship plans then learn how to say so...

À l'avenir, je voudrais ... = In the future, I'd like...

... to become rich:	devenir riche
... to get married:	me marier
... to have children:	avoir des enfants

Je ne veux pas me marier tout de suite. = I don't want to get married right away.

Je voudrais habiter dans une grande maison. = I'd like to live in a big house.

I'd like to propose...

...that you take another look over this page so it all comes trippingly off the tongue. It's a bit embarrassing talking about relationships in French lessons, but you'll just have to get used to it.

Social Issues and Equality

Unemployment, equal ops, gender and race issues — it's enough to make you want to wave around a big banner. Try a verse of 'We shall not, we shall not be moved' — simply superb for revision morale.

Notre société n'est pas égale — Our society isn't equal

Des gens sont méchants avec moi parce que je viens d'Afrique.

= Some people are mean to me because I come from Africa.

I am a girl / a guy: je suis une fille / un garçon
I am younger / older: je suis plus jeune / plus âgé(e)

Ce n'est pas facile d'avoir une nationalité différente.

= It's not easy to have a different nationality.

La violence et le vandalisme — Violence and vandalism

Il y a beaucoup de violence dans ma ville.

= There is lots of violence in my town.

vandalism: vandalisme

C'est effrayant.

= It's terrifying.

hit: battu(e)

En rentrant à la maison une fois j'ai été menacé(e).

= On the way home once I was threatened.

alone: seul(e)

J'évite de sortir la nuit.

= I avoid going out at night.

Les effets du chômage — The effects of unemployment

Il y a beaucoup de gens sans travail dans ma ville.

= There are lots of unemployed people in my town.

homeless people: SDF (sans domicile fixe)
disadvantaged people: personnes défavorisées

Fromage au chômage.

Il est au chômage depuis deux ans.

= He's been out of work for two years.

Sans argent, il est difficile de trouver un logement.

= Without money, it's difficult to find housing.

J'ai peur de ne pas trouver un boulot.

= I'm scared I won't find a job.

Sorry, a bit bleak, this page...

Hardly a barrel of laughs, was it, and quite a tricky one to boot. Try to learn some of the more complex sentences off by heart. You'll be surprised how this will help you in the assessments.

Feeling Ill

Pain, illness and suffering — more fun and frolics from those full-of-glee examiners. I suppose if setting the exams every year is as mind-numbing as taking them, it's not surprising they aren't too chirpy.

Comment ça va? — How are you?

Je suis malade. = I feel ill.

Je ne me sens pas bien. = I don't feel well.

Je dois aller voir le médecin. = I need to go to see the doctor.

to the hospital: à l'hôpital (masc.)
to the chemist's: à la pharmacie

Où as-tu mal? — Where does it hurt?

Here's how you say what bit hurts...

You can use 'j'ai mal à' with any part of your body that's hurting...

J'ai mal à l'estomac. = I have stomach ache.

a headache: mal à la tête
backache: mal au dos
a sore throat: mal à la gorge
earache: mal à l'oreille

Use 'au' for 'le' words, 'à la' for 'la' words, 'à l'' for words starting with a vowel or a silent 'h', and 'aux' for plurals.

LA TÊTE: THE HEAD

the nose:	le nez
the eye:	l'œil (masc.)
the eyes:	les yeux (masc.)
the ear:	l'oreille (fem.)
the mouth:	la bouche
the teeth:	les dents (fem.)

Mon doigt me fait mal. = My finger hurts / has been hurting.

My head: Ma tête
My arms: Mes bras (masc.)
My ears: Mes oreilles (fem.)
hurt (plural): font mal

LE CORPS: THE BODY

the head:	la tête
the throat:	la gorge
the back:	le dos
the foot:	le pied
the leg:	la jambe
the finger:	le doigt
the hand:	la main
the arm:	le bras

Je me suis cassé le bras. = I've broken my arm.

J'ai un rhume. = I have a cold.

a cough: une toux
flu: la grippe
a temperature: de la fièvre

Pouvez-vous me donner quelque chose? — Can you give me something?

Pouvez-vous me donner un médicament? = Can you give me some medicine?

some plasters: des sparadraps (masc.)
some tablets: des comprimés (masc.)
some aspirin: de l'aspirine (fem.)

Ça va mieux. = I feel better.

Ça va bien. = I feel well.

What do you call the cold part of a French house...

...un rhume. This feeling ill vocab might easily come up in one of your speaking or listening tasks. Admittedly, it might not. Much in the same way that Daniel Craig may or may not propose to me this year. There's no way of knowing — so you'd best keep learning this stuff and I'll keep hoping.

Health and Health Issues

These next two pages are a bit like PSHE in French — you lucky, lucky people. You probably have an opinion on this stuff already. Some of the French vocab and expressions are a bit tricky though.

Qu'est-ce que tu fais pour rester en bonne santé?

What do you do to stay healthy?

Pour rester en bonne santé ...

= To stay healthy ...

I eat lots of vegetables:	je mange beaucoup de légumes.
I don't eat chocolate:	je ne mange pas de chocolat.
I drink water often:	je bois souvent de l'eau.

Je fais beaucoup de sport pour ...

= I play a lot of sport to ...

stay fit:	rester en forme.
have fun:	m'amuser.

Je ne fais rien parce que ...

= I do nothing because ...

I'm lazy:	je suis paresseux / paresseuse.
I don't have time:	je n'ai pas le temps.
I'm already perfect:	je suis déjà parfait(e).

Je suis au régime. = I'm on a diet.

L'obésité est un grand problème

Obesity is a big problem

Here's how to give your opinion on expanding waistlines...

Il est triste de voir des enfants très gros. = It's sad to see very fat children.

awful: affreux — *really:* vraiment

À mon avis, c'est la faute de la publicité. In my opinion, it's the fault of advertising.

of society: de la société — *of the parents:* des parents

Beaucoup de gens ne mangent pas suffisamment

A lot of people don't eat enough

...and on tiny waistlines...

Beaucoup de gens pensent qu'il faut être maigre comme les vedettes.

= Lots of people think you have to be thin like celebrities.

Ce n'est pas sain. = It's not healthy.

Pour être en bonne santé, il faut bien manger. = To be healthy, you need to eat well.

Get your 5 a day. No, not 5 doughnuts...

Seriously, there's loads of stuff on this page that could easily come up somewhere in the assessments. Some of the 'opinions' stuff is quite tricky, but you need to be ready for anything.

Health and Health Issues

Drugs, booze and fags. Enjoy.

Qu'est-ce que tu penses du tabac?

What do you think of tobacco?

This stuff's relevant for drugs and alcohol — so learn the vocab in the pale boxes too.

Je ne fume pas. = I don't smoke.

J'aime fumer. = I like smoking.

Je sais que ce n'est pas sain, mais je pense que c'est cool. = I know it's unhealthy, but I think it's cool.

Fumer, c'est affreux. = Smoking is horrible.

Alcohol: L'alcool (masc.)

Beaucoup de jeunes boivent trop d'alcool. = Lots of young people drink too much alcohol.

smoke: fument   take drugs: se droguent

A mon avis, se droguer est très dangereux. = In my opinion, taking drugs is very dangerous.

alcohol: l'alcool   tobacco: le tabac

Je ne fume plus — I don't smoke any more

J'ai arreté de fumer parce que j'ai des problèmes de santé. = I stopped because I've got health problems.

it's too expensive: c'est trop cher

drink: bois

Mon copain / ma copine n'aime pas quand je fume. = My boyfriend / girlfriend doesn't like it when I smoke.

La drogue dans le sport — Drugs in sport

Often a big talking-point for the French, this. Especially when the Tour de France is on.

La drogue est un problème dans le cyclisme. = Drugs are a problem in cycling.

football: le football

Performance-enhancing revision guides are OK...

There's loads you might want to say about these exciting topics, but learning the stuff on this page is a good start. Think about what else you might want to say, write it down, and practise it.

Revision Summary

These questions are here to make sure you know your stuff. Work through them and look up the answers to any tough ones you're struggling with. Keep practising them all again and again. Do I sound like a broken record yet... Hope so. I've always wondered what that might be like.

1) You're making fruit salad for a party. Think of as many different fruits as you can to put in it — and write down at least 5 in French. Make a list (in French) of 5 drinks for the party too.

2) Your hosts are offering you more chocolate cake. Decline politely and say the meal was delicious. Offer to pass your hostess the milk for her coffee.

3) Write down how you'd say that you like vegetables but don't like sausages. You don't eat meat and you're hungry.

4) You're telling your host family all about your home life. Say that you walk the dog, do the shopping and wash the car. Tell them that you earn pocket money for helping out at home.

5) How would you tell your name, age and birthday to someone you've just met?

6) Describe three of your friends and say how old they are. Comment on the colour of their eyes and spell their names out loud.

7) Tell your French penfriend what relations you have — including how many aunts, uncles etc.

8) Your animal-loving friend has six rabbits, a bird, a guinea pig and two cats. How could she say what these are in French?

9) Imagine that you are a boring, mean and hardworking person who has a bad sense of humour. How would you say all this in French?

10) Write three sentences about the personalities of two of your favourite celebrities.

11) In your opinion, what three qualities should a good friend have? Finish the following sentence: "À mon avis, un bon ami / une bonne amie doit..."

12) Isabelle says: "J'ai un petit ami qui s'appelle François. On s'entend bien. Nous sommes meilleurs amis. On ne se dispute jamais. François est gentil, sympa et plein de vie, et il est toujours là pour moi." (Sickening.) What did she say in English?

13) Write a short paragraph about violence and vandalism in your town.

14) Do the same as in Q.13 but for unemployment... Sorry.

15) How would you say you have each of these ailments in French?
a) stomach ache b) headache c) a cold d) flu e) a broken arm

16) Are you healthy? Why / why not? Write a couple of sentences about it in French.

17) Imagine you used to smoke but now you've stopped. Explain why in French.

Sports and Hobbies

Examiners don't believe in couch potatoes — there's always loads in the exams about sports and hobbies.

Est-ce que tu fais du sport? — Do you do any sport?

There's a chance sports and hobbies could come up in the speaking and writing assessments. Even if you're no demon on the pitch, you need to be good at talking about all things sport in French.

VERBS FOR SPORTS

to go fishing:	aller à la pêche
to run:	courir
to cycle:	faire du cyclisme
to swim:	nager
to ski:	faire du ski
to play:	jouer
to walk, hike:	faire une randonnée
to ice skate:	patiner

PLACES YOU CAN DO SPORTS

sports centre:	le centre sportif
swimming pool:	la piscine
sports field:	le terrain de sport
park:	le parc
ice rink:	la patinoire
mountains:	les montagnes (fem.)

NAMES OF SPORTS

basketball:	le basket
football:	le football
tennis:	le tennis
table tennis:	le tennis de table
horse riding:	l'équitation (fem.)
skateboarding:	le skate
swimming:	la natation
ice skating:	le patinage
snowboarding:	le surf des neiges
water sports:	les sports nautiques
winter sports:	les sports d'hiver

Je joue au basket. = I play basketball.

Oui, je fais beaucoup de sport parce que ... = Yes, I do a lot of sport because...

it's free:	c'est gratuit.
it's good for your health:	c'est bon pour la santé.

Non, je ne fais pas de sport parce que ... = No, I don't do any sport because...

I'm not sporty:	je ne suis pas sportif / sportive.
it doesn't interest me:	ça ne m'intéresse pas.

Est-ce que tu as un passe-temps? — Do you have a hobby?

There are other things to do apart from sports — that's where these tasty selections come into play.

MUSICAL INSTRUMENTS

flute:	la flûte
drum kit:	la batterie
guitar:	la guitare
trumpet:	la trompette
piano:	le piano
violin:	le violon

To see how to use present tense verbs with different people, see pages 92-93.

VERBS FOR INDOOR ACTIVITIES

to dance:	danser
to sing:	chanter
to collect:	collectionner
to read:	lire

MUSICAL WORDS

band, group:	le groupe
CD:	le CD, le disque compact
instrument:	l'instrument (masc.)
concert:	le concert

OTHER IMPORTANT WORDS

film:	le film
performance:	le spectacle
play:	la pièce (de théâtre)
reading:	la lecture

If music's what you're into, see page 30.

Get on your hobby-horse...

Blummin' great. Not only do you have to do sport in PE, you have to talk about it in French. Even if you hate sport and music, you'll have to pretend you do something. And you'll need to know the others when you hear them. Luckily most of them sound more or less like the English. Phew.

Sports and Hobbies

What you do in your free time comes up somewhere in the assessments every year. You have to be able to write about what you get up to, and give opinions of other hobbies. It's must-learn stuff. Yeah it is.

Qu'est-ce que tu fais pendant ton temps libre? — What do you do in your free time?

Sport and music are really big topics in the assessments.

Je joue **au football** **le week-end**. = I play football at weekends.

basketball:	au basket
tennis:	au tennis

every day:	chaque jour
every week:	chaque semaine
twice a month:	deux fois par mois

For more about times, see pages 2–3.

IMPORTANT: 'à' and 'de'

If you're talking about games, use 'jouer à', but with instruments, it's 'jouer de'.

à + le	= au	de + le	= du
à + la	= à la	de + la	= de la
à + l'	= à l'	de + l'	= de l'
à + les	= aux	de + les	= des
Je joue au basket.		Je joue de la guitare.	

Je joue **du piano**. = I play the piano.

See previous page for more musical instruments.

Est-ce que tu aimes le football? — Do you like football?

Here's how to say what you think of different hobbies — learn these phrases, even if you don't really care.

Je trouve **le football** **fantastique**. = I think football is fantastic.

the cinema:	le cinéma
hiking:	les randonnées

exciting:	passionnant(e)(s)
interesting:	intéressant(e)(s)

Oui, j'adore **le football**. = Yes, I love football.

More options on page 26.

Je n'aime pas **courir**, *parce que c'est* **difficile**. = I don't like running, because it's difficult.

passing the ball: passer le ballon

boring: ennuyeux ← Always use the masculine form after "c'est".

Le tennis de table *est* **bon** *parce que c'est* **facile**. = Table tennis is good because it's easy.

iceskating: le patinage — *horrible:* affreux — *dangerous:* dangereux

More on opinions on pages 7-8.

Free time, expensive hobbies...

There's important stuff on this page — you need to be able to say what you do in your free time and why. Make sure you remember when it's 'jouer à' and when it's 'jouer de'. While you're at it, learn all this opinion stuff for saying what you think about sports and hobbies. Fu-un...

Television

Ah, the telly. You might have to listen to people talk about television in the exam, or you may need to talk about it in the speaking assessment. You never know, so make sure this is part of your repertoire.

Qu'est-ce que tu aimes regarder à la télé? — What do you like to watch on TV?

Basically, this stuff's all really handy.

Quelles émissions est-ce que tu aimes regarder ?

Which books: Quels livres

to read: lire

= Which TV programmes do you like to watch?

to listen to: écouter   to read: lire

Put what you like to watch, listen to or read here.

J'aime regarder Westenders .

= I like to watch Westenders.

a documentary:	un documentaire
a soap:	un feuilleton
a film:	un film
a play:	une pièce (de théâtre)
a show:	un spectacle
an advertisement:	une publicité

documentaries:	des documentaires
soaps:	des feuilletons
films:	des films
plays:	des pièces de théâtre
shows:	des spectacles
advertisements:	des publicités

For more about giving opinions, see pages 7-8.

Je voudrais regarder ...

= I would like to watch ...

L'émission commence à vingt heures le mercredi soir .

For more info. about time and days of the week, see page 2.

= The programme starts at 8pm on Wednesday evenings.

Qu'est-ce que tu as fait récemment? — What have you done recently?

This bit of past tense looks really impressive — and it's always good for a little bit o' French banter...

For more about times and dates, see pages 2–3.

J'ai vu Amélie récemment .

= I saw Amélie recently.

heard: écouté
read: lu

the radio: la radio
the new song by Take This: la nouvelle chanson de Take This

last week:	la semaine dernière
two weeks ago:	il y a deux semaines
a month ago:	il y a un mois

Before you reach for the remote...

The French often call TV 'le petit écran' (= 'the small screen'). What do they call the cinema (yes, apart from 'cinéma', smarty-pants)? Yep, 'le grand écran'. Try to think of particular programmes you like to watch, and explain why you like them. It's a surefire route to success...

Talking About the Plot

Books, films, telly programmes — you may have to discuss things you've read, seen or heard recently. It sounds quite scary, even in English, but it's really simple if you learn these easy phrases...

J'ai lu, J'ai vu, J'ai entendu... — I read, I saw, I heard...

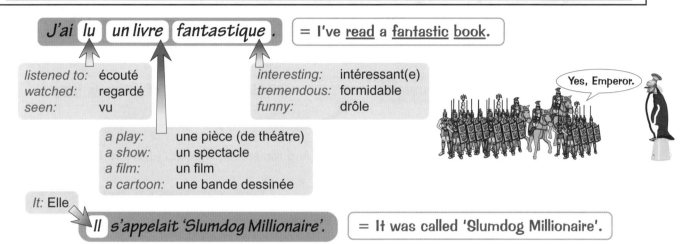

J'ai lu un livre fantastique. = I've read a fantastic book.

listened to:	écouté
watched:	regardé
seen:	vu

interesting:	intéressant(e)
tremendous:	formidable
funny:	drôle

a play:	une pièce (de théâtre)
a show:	un spectacle
a film:	un film
a cartoon:	une bande dessinée

Yes, Emperor.

It: Elle

Il s'appelait 'Slumdog Millionaire'. = It was called 'Slumdog Millionaire'.

Parle-moi du film... — Tell me about the film...

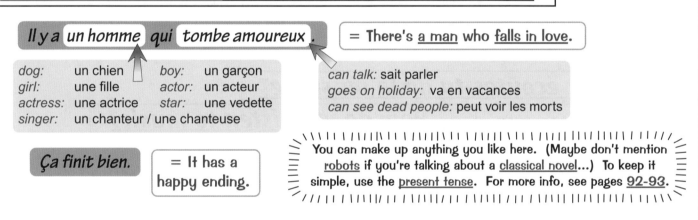

Il y a un homme qui tombe amoureux. = There's a man who falls in love.

dog:	un chien	*boy:*	un garçon
girl:	une fille	*actor:*	un acteur
actress:	une actrice	*star:*	une vedette
singer:	un chanteur / une chanteuse		

can talk: sait parler
goes on holiday: va en vacances
can see dead people: peut voir les morts

Ça finit bien. = It has a happy ending.

You can make up anything you like here. (Maybe don't mention robots if you're talking about a classical novel...) To keep it simple, use the present tense. For more info, see pages 92-93.

Comment as-tu trouvé le spectacle? — How did you find the show?

Opinions go down really well at GCSE French — so you need to learn this stuff... and get an opinion.

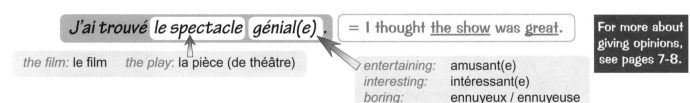

J'ai trouvé le spectacle génial(e). = I thought the show was great.

the film: le film *the play:* la pièce (de théâtre)

entertaining:	amusant(e)
interesting:	intéressant(e)
boring:	ennuyeux / ennuyeuse
fantastic:	fantastique

For more about giving opinions, see pages 7-8.

Lu, vu and entendu... that's a lot of ooos...

I really should be writing song lyrics for Kylie or Take That, but I'm far too busy writing a French book. Once again, it's all about me. They'll be making a film of my life soon, called... um...

Music

Treasons, stratagems and spoils. That's what Shakespeare said you're fit for if you don't like music. Learn how to say what music you're into. If you are fit for those things, there's no harm in making it up.

Qu'est-ce que tu aimes comme musique? — What kind of music do you like?

All fairly basic stuff this. You need to find interesting ways of talking about your musical tastes though.

Ma musique préférée, c'est la musique jazz. = My favourite type of music is jazz.

pop rock danse classique rap

It's really good if you can explain exactly what you like. (And remember, it doesn't have to be true.)

very good: très bon / bonne
splendid: merveilleux / merveilleuse
interesting: intéressant / intéressante

More describing words on pages 80-81.

Je trouve Beethoven vraiment chouette. = I find Beethoven really great.

all rap music: toute la musique rap
Johnny Hallyday's music: la musique de Johnny Hallyday
French music: la musique française

It's good to talk about any foreign music you've heard, too — you can bet your French teacher loves Europop.

Comment écoutes-tu de la musique? — How do you listen to music?

This bit's how to say where and how you listen to music.

J'écoute de la musique sur mon lecteur mp3. = I listen to music on my mp3 player.

in my bedroom: dans ma chambre
on my mobile phone: sur mon téléphone portable

To play an instrument is 'jouer d'un instrument'

Je joue du piano depuis l'âge de six ans. = I've played the piano since the age of six.

the guitar: de la guitare
the keyboard: du clavier
the drums: de la batterie

Talking about age is on page 17.

See page 26 for more musical instruments.

Je fais partie d'un groupe. = I play in a band.

Every French teacher loves a bit of Johnny...

If music comes up in one of the assessments, and you haven't got much to say, you could try: 'J'aimerais jouer du piano' (= 'I'd like to...'), and then give a reason. Gotta be better than nothing.

Famous People

Now this choice of topic seems a tad weird to me, but apparently you are supposed to be fascinated by celebs. So much so that you want to talk about them in French with your exchange partners...

Quelles vedettes aimes-tu? — Which stars do you like?

This is the same straightforward stuff that you use to talk about you and your family.

WHO — *Je trouve Beyoncé Knowles fantastique.* = I think Beyoncé Knowles is fantastic.

WHAT — *C'est une chanteuse américaine célèbre.* = She is a famous American singer.

WHY — *J'aimerais pouvoir chanter comme elle.* = I'd like to be able to sing like her.

Extra marks for style

La journée d'une vedette — A day in the life of a star

You may be asked to put yourself in someone else's French-speaking shoes — when you're imagining your daily life as a celebrity, these phrases may come in useful...

Le matin, j'écris de nouvelles chansons. = In the morning, I write new songs.

a book about my life: un livre sur ma vie

Tous les soirs, je mange dans un bon restaurant. = Every evening, I eat in a good restaurant.

Every day: Chaque jour
Often: Souvent

other famous people: d'autres gens célèbres
beautiful women: de belles femmes

Je sors avec des acteurs bien connus. = I go out with well-known actors.

Vous aimez être célèbre? — Do you like being famous?

If they ask you to write an interview with a celeb, here are some useful phrases:

Oui, j'aime être célèbre parce que ... = Yes, I like being famous because ...

I've got lots of friends: j'ai beaucoup d'amis.
I have lots of money: j'ai beaucoup d'argent.
I am able to travel: je peux voyager.

Non, je déteste être célèbre parce que ... = No, I hate being famous because ...

I don't have a private life: je n'ai pas de vie privée.
I'm always in the papers: je suis toujours dans les journaux.
I can't go to the supermarket: je ne peux pas aller au supermarché.

I'm your number one fan...

This page gives you the freedom to give your opinion on celebrities and their influence in society — all in a foreign language. It's tricky stuff, but master this and your French will be fabulous.

New Technology

Ah, computers. They've even found their way into GCSE French.

Je suis souvent sur l'ordinateur — I'm often on the computer

Computers are a new favourite with the examiners (they've only just discovered the existence of the internet), so there's a fairly good chance that you'll have to give your views on technology:

J'envoie beaucoup d'emails. = I send lots of emails.

emails: de courriers électroniques *text messsages:* de textos *faxes:* de fax

There are two French words for email: 'l'email' and 'le courrier électronique'.

computer: ordinateur *mobile phone:* portable

J'utilise mon appareil photo souvent et je partage des photos avec mes amis.

= I often use my camera and I share photos with my friends.

talk to my friends: parler avec mes amis *shop:* faire des courses

Avec l'internet, c'est plus facile de faire mes devoirs.

= With the internet, it's easier to do my homework.

nice: agréable

Ce n'est pas sain de passer trop de temps sur l'ordinateur.

= It's not healthy to spend too much time on the computer.

Je vais mettre ça sur mon site — I'll put that on my website

In your written assessment, you might be asked to write about your life in a blog or personal web page. No need to panic — it's just like any other 'day in the life' stuff, and will probably end up looking something like this:

Manchester 25/02/2009 19h20

Aujourd'hui j'ai passé une journée très agréable. Je suis allée voir des amis au pays de Galles avec ma famille.

À midi on a mangé du poulet rôti et de la tarte au chocolat. C'était délicieux. Plus tard, nous nous sommes promenés dans un joli petit village.

Regardez les photos ici: 

Today I had a very nice day. I went to see some friends in Wales with my family.

At midday we ate roast chicken and chocolate tart. It was delicious. Later we went for a walk in a pretty little village.

Look at the photos here: 

The blogger describes what he/she has done today in the perfect tense. See pages 95-97.

Soon we won't even need carrier pigeons...

Never mind that this technology's been around since before you were born, the examiners still think it's fresh and new. If it doesn't crop up somewhere I'll eat my network cable, so get it learnt.

Shopping

This section gives you all the bog-standard stuff you need to know when you're out and about shopping.

Où est...? — Where is...?

A dead handy question, this one.

Où est **la boulangerie**, s'il vous plaît?

the till: la caisse

= Where is the baker's, please?

D'autres magasins — Other shops

grocer's:	l'épicerie (fem.)	*bookshop:*	la librairie
hypermarket:	l'hypermarché (masc.)	*cake shop:*	la pâtisserie
newsagent:	le tabac	*sweet shop:*	la confiserie
perfume shop:	la parfumerie	*delicatessen:*	la charcuterie
jeweller's:	la bijouterie	*butcher's:*	la boucherie

À quelle heure...? — What time...?

You need these useful sentences to talk about when shops are open or closed.

À quelle heure est-ce que le magasin **ouvre** ?

= What time does the shop open?

close: ferme

For times, see page 2.

Le supermarché ouvre à **neuf heures** .

= The supermarket opens at nine o'clock.

Tous les magasins ferment à **six heures** .

= All the shops shut at six o'clock.

Allons faire les magasins! — Let's go shopping!

Here's how to talk about your personal shopping habits:

Le week-end, je suis souvent **au centre commercial** .

= At the weekend, I'm often at the shopping centre.

in town: en ville
in my favourite shop: dans ma boutique préférée

J'aime **essayer beaucoup de vêtements** .

= I like to try on lots of clothes.

window shopping: regarder les vitrines.

J'attends les soldes pour avoir des réductions.

= I wait for the sales so I can get discounts.

Hypermarché — an excited market...

You might have to talk about where things are and when they open in your speaking assessment — you'd be daft not to learn it. If this stuff doesn't come up, then I'm a wombat. Get these sentences learnt, along with the names of as many shops as you can possibly squeeze up there...

Shopping

Don't go reckoning you'll get through your exam without ever having to mention (or recognise someone else mentioning) buying stuff. Everything on this page is here because you need it. Trust me and learn it.

Est-ce que je peux vous aider? — Can I help you?

Say what you'd like using 'Je voudrais...'

1kg: un kilo   *a litre:* un litre   *a packet:* un paquet

Je voudrais cinq cents grammes de sucre, s'il vous plaît. = I'd like 500g of sugar, please.

The shop assistant might say:

Autre chose? = Anything else?

C'est tout? = Is that everything?

See page 1 for more on numbers.

You could reply:

Non, merci. = No, thank you.

Non, je voudrais aussi des pommes de terre, s'il vous plaît. = No, I'd like some potatoes as well, please.

two apples: deux pommes (fem.)
three pears: trois poires (fem.)

Est-ce que vous avez...? — Do you have...?

It's useful to know these phrases in case they pop up in your listening exam.

Excusez-moi, avez-vous du pain? = Excuse me, do you have any bread?

milk: du lait   *cheese:* du fromage   *eggs:* des œufs (masc.)   *bananas:* des bananes (fem.)

Oui, le voilà. = Yes, there it is.

it: le / la

Non, nous n'en avons pas. = No, we don't have any.

Je voudrais un peu de fromage. = I'd like a bit of cheese.

lots of: beaucoup de   a slice of: une tranche de

Je voudrais quelques pommes. = I'd like some apples.

See page 13 for more on food.

Ça fait combien? — How much is that?

French money's easy. There are 100 cents in a euro, like there are 100 pence in a pound.

This is what you'd see on a French price tag:

Ça fait cinq euros cinquante.

This is how you say the price. = That'll be 5 euros 50 cents

bank card: carte bancaire

Est-ce que je peux payer par carte de crédit? = Can I pay with a credit card?

Splash out, buy a boat...

Money and shop talk are pretty important, especially for those nasty (and often embarrassing) speaking assessment thingies. Don't worry. Simply revise. And be happy. (Oh, and just in case it comes up in the listening exam — the French don't pronounce the 'f' in 'des œufs'.)

Shopping

Shopping for a bunch of bananas is all well and good, but shopping for clothes could pop up in your exams — when someone in the listening exam is banging on about the fab pair of socks they just purchased online.

Je fais des économies... — I'm saving up...

Knowing this useful vocab about pocket money will make your shop talk more interesting...

Je reçois dix euros d'argent de poche par mois.

£5: cinq livres

week: semaine

= I get ten euros pocket money a month.

I'd like to buy: Je voudrais acheter

J'achète des vêtements avec mon argent de poche.

make-up:	du maquillage
computer games:	des jeux vidéo (masc.)

= I buy clothes with my pocket money.

Les vêtements — Clothing

Most of these clothes are everyday items — so you need to know them.

J'aime cette chemise. = I like this shirt.

Je n'aime pas ce manteau. = I don't like this coat.

shirt:	la chemise
trousers:	le pantalon
jeans:	le jean
shorts:	le short
dress:	la robe
jacket:	la veste
skirt:	la jupe
jumper:	le pull

sock:	la chaussette
shoe:	la chaussure
trainer:	le basket
sandal:	la sandale
hat:	le chapeau
tie:	la cravate
glove:	le gant
watch:	la montre

handbag:	le sac à main
purse:	le porte-monnaie
wallet:	le portefeuille
pyjamas:	le pyjama
raincoat:	l'imperméable (masc.)
casual jacket:	le blouson
swimming costume:	le maillot de bain

Le chapeau

Le tee-shirt

La jupe

They might ask what colour you want — quelle couleur...?

Colours crop up all over the place. The colour goes after the noun, and agrees with it (see pages 80-81).

Je voudrais un pantalon bleu.

= I'd like a pair of blue trousers.

Je voudrais une jupe verte.

= I'd like a green skirt.

COLOURS: les couleurs (fem.)

black:	noir(e)	*brown:*	brun(e)
white:	blanc(he)	*orange:*	orange
red:	rouge	*pink:*	rose
yellow:	jaune	*light blue:*	bleu clair
green:	vert(e)	*dark blue:*	bleu foncé
blue:	bleu(e)		

So, how do you say "fluorescent lime PVC flares" again...

It's common sense — just don't forget your clothes. Some of them are dead easy — le pyjama, le pull, le short etc. Others need a bit more effort. It'll be worth it, though. Honestly.

Shopping

Here's another pretty important page of lovely French shopping stuff — last one though. Result...

Je voudrais... — I would like...

Make sure you're really comfortable with 'Je voudrais' — you'll be needing it all the time.

Je voudrais un pantalon s'il vous plaît.

For clothing, see page 35.

= I'd like a pair of trousers please.

Je prends la taille quarante-quatre.

= I'm size 44.

Je voudrais un échange, s'il vous plaît.

= I'd like to exchange this, please.

CONTINENTAL SIZES

size: la taille

dress size 8 / 10 / 12 / 14 / 16: 36 / 38 / 40 / 42 / 44

shoe size 5 / 6 / 7 / 8 / 9 / 10: 38 / 39 / 41 / 42 / 43 / 44

Je cherche... — I'm looking for...

Details are good — try to learn all the bits of these phrases so you don't get caught out in the listening...

brown: brun(e) *blue:* bleu(e)

Je cherche un pull en laine rose.

= I'm looking for a pink woollen jumper.

a jacket: une veste

cotton: en coton

'Ce', 'cette' etc. are on page 89.

Je voudrais essayer cette jupe.

= I'd like to try this skirt on.

these trousers: ce pantalon

It's good to talk about the latest trends too...

Les jupes courtes sont très à la mode.

= Short skirts are very fashionable.

Est-ce que vous le prenez? — Will you be taking that?

To buy or not to buy — that is the question. Learn these useful phrases too:

Je prends le pull.

= I'll take the jumper.

Je ne prends pas la jupe. Je n'aime pas la couleur.

It's too small: C'est trop petit.

It's a bit old-fashioned: C'est un peu démodé.

= I'll leave the skirt. I don't like the colour.

Will you be taking that? — No, I was going to pay...

There's loads of shopping language here that'll come in really handy. Learn as much of this as you can. And remember — as long as you know your stuff, you'll do fine in your GCSE. Simple.

Inviting People Out

A brief guide to having fun in French: 1) get someone to agree to do some fun stuff 2) come to a mutual agreement about what you're going to do 3) organise a party to celebrate all the fun...

Sortons — Let's go out

These are all really useful phrases for the assessments, so get them learnt.

Using the 'nous' form here means 'let's' — see page 101.

Allons au théâtre. = Let's go to the theatre.

to the swimming pool: à la piscine *to the park:* au parc

Oui, je veux bien. = Yes, I'd love to.

Good idea!: Bonne idée!
Great!: Super!
OK: D'accord

Non, merci. = No, thank you.

I'm sorry, I can't: Je suis désolé(e), je ne peux pas.
I don't have enough money: Je n'ai pas assez d'argent.

À quelle heure commence le spectacle? = When does the performance start?

finish: finit *the film:* le film *the match:* le match

Il commence à huit heures et finit à dix heures. = It starts at 8.00 and finishes at 10.00.

J'organise une surprise-partie... — I'm organising a surprise party...

Party planning. In French. Could be useful...

La fête est chez moi samedi prochain. = The party's at my house next Saturday.

at Sophie's: chez Sophie

C'est pour fêter mon anniversaire. = It's to celebrate my birthday.

On va écouter de la musique et manger une pizza. = We're going to listen to music and eat a pizza.

to watch movies: regarder des films
to dance: danser

sweets: des bonbons
chocolate: du chocolat

For more foods, see page 13.

Veux-tu venir? = Do you want to come?

Oops, not such a surprise any more...

It seems odd to me that they want you to talk about a surprise party you're organising — if you tell people, it's not much of a surprise. Anyway, avoid potentially nasty surprises by learning this.

Going Out

This stuff about buying tickets, opening times and where things are is essential — you need to be able to talk about it for your speaking assessments, or understand it in the listening exam.

...près d'ici? — ...near here?

Est-ce qu'il y a un théâtre près d'ici? = Is there a theatre near here?

a sports field: un terrain de sport *a bowling alley:* un bowling *a cinema:* un cinéma

play tennis: jouer au tennis *go for walks:* se promener

Peut-on nager près d'ici? = Can we swim near here?

'Combien ça coûte?' — 'How much does it cost?'

Combien coûte l'entrée à la piscine ? = How much does it cost to go swimming?

bowling: au bowling
to the cinema: au cinéma

Ça coûte deux euros l'heure. = It costs 2 euros per hour.

Combien coûte un billet ? = How much does one ticket cost?

How much do two tickets cost?: Combien coûtent deux billets ?

Plural endings.

Un billet coûte cinq euros. = One ticket costs 5 euros.

two tickets: deux billets

Je voudrais un billet , s'il vous plaît. = I'd like one ticket, please.

Ouvert(e) ou fermé(e)? — Open or closed?

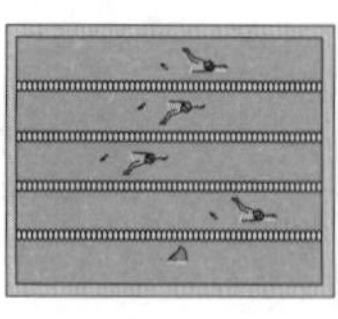

À quelle heure est-ce que la piscine est ouverte ? = What time is the swimming pool open?

the sports centre: le centre sportif *closed:* fermé(e)

Elle ouvre à neuf heures et demie et ferme à cinq heures . = It opens at half past nine and closes at five o'clock.

'Il' for a masculine place.

For other places, see page 57.

French makes my head spin — I feel "d'ici"...

This stuff could come up in your speaking assessment or listening exam — you need to be able to understand it all... So don't just sit there, let's get to it — get into gear and get down to it.

Going Out

Finally... something fun to stick on the French revision schedule — films and trips to the cinema.

Je suis allé(e) au cinéma — I went to the cinema

There's a chance you'll have to mention what you did last weekend. Make sure you have a decent answer.

my parents: mes parents *some friends:* des ami(e)s

J'ai regardé un film avec un ami. = I watched a film with a friend.

I went shopping: J'ai fait des courses *I went clubbing:* Je suis allé(e) en boîte (de nuit)

Après nous avons mangé au restaurant. = Afterwards we ate at a restaurant.

In the evening: Le soir
Later: Plus tard

For more on talking about the past, see pages 95-97.

Est-ce que le film était bien? — Was the film good?

You've got to be able to say whether you thought the film was any good — it's dead easy.

C'était quelle sorte de film? = What sort of film was it?

C'était un film d'horreur. = It was a horror film.

romantic:	d'amour	*comedy:*	comique	*war:*	de guerre
sci-fi:	de science-fiction	*adventure:*	d'aventures	*detective:*	policier

Qu'est-ce que tu as pensé du film? = What did you think of the film?

of the performance: du spectacle
of the play: de la pièce (de théâtre)
of the concert: du concert

To find out more about giving opinions, see pages 7-8.

Le film était bien. = The film was good.

very good: très bien
bad: mauvais(e)

Je n'ai pas aimé la fin. = I didn't like the ending.

the story: l'histoire

I watched Jaws, but I didn't like 'la fin...'

A fair bit to learn here. But as long as you can give your opinion on whatever you've seen or done, it's a big piece of gâteau... That's all I have to say. There's no more advice at this point.

Revision Summary

These questions are here to make sure you know your stuff. Work through them all and check the ones you couldn't do. Look back through the section to find the answers, then have another go at knocking those pesky troublesome ones right out of the parking lot. And (eventually) voilà.

1) What is the French for each of these sports? What's the French for the place where you would do them? a) football b) swimming c) snowboarding d) ice-skating
2) Write down as many French words as you can to do with playing or listening to music.
3) Say that you go swimming at the weekend and riding on Tuesdays.
4) You like watching films and soaps on TV. Tonight you'd like to watch a documentary that starts at nine o'clock. How would you say this in French?
5) Think of a film you saw recently and one you saw a month ago, and say this in French. (You don't have to translate the film titles into French.)
6) You have just watched an interesting programme. Say this in French. Then tell me its title and what it was about.
7) What sort of music do you like? Where do you listen to it? Give your answers in French.
8) Nadine thinks she's fallen in love with Robbie Williams. Write a short paragraph to her in French saying what you think about him.
9) Now imagine you're Robbie. Do you like being famous? Why? (Give two reasons.)
10) Think of one good and one bad thing about the internet and then write your views down in at least two French sentences.
11) You're out of bread. How do you ask where the baker's is and whether it's open?
12) What are the French names for: a) a newsagent b) a cake shop c) a butcher's d) a bookshop e) a sweet shop f) a perfume shop
13) Where do you prefer shopping? Why?
14) A shop assistant asks you 'Est-ce que je peux vous aider?' and later 'Voulez-vous autre chose?' What do these two questions mean in English? How would you answer them?
15) You want to buy a brown jumper in size 38. How do you say this to the shop assistant?
16) Imagine you're having a surprise party for your birthday. Describe what you'll be getting up to in no more than 3 French sentences.
17) Tu veux aller voir un film. Le film commence à vingt et une heures et finit à vingt-deux heures trente. Un billet coûte cinq euros. What does this mean in English?
18) Describe in French a show, a film or a play that you've seen recently. (3 phrases max.)

Holiday Destinations

You need to know about countries and nationalities for describing yourself or your holiday plans in your speaking and writing tasks, or for understanding descriptions of people in the reading and listening papers.

D'où viens-tu? — Where do you come from?

Learn this phrase off by heart — if the country you're from isn't here, check in a dictionary...

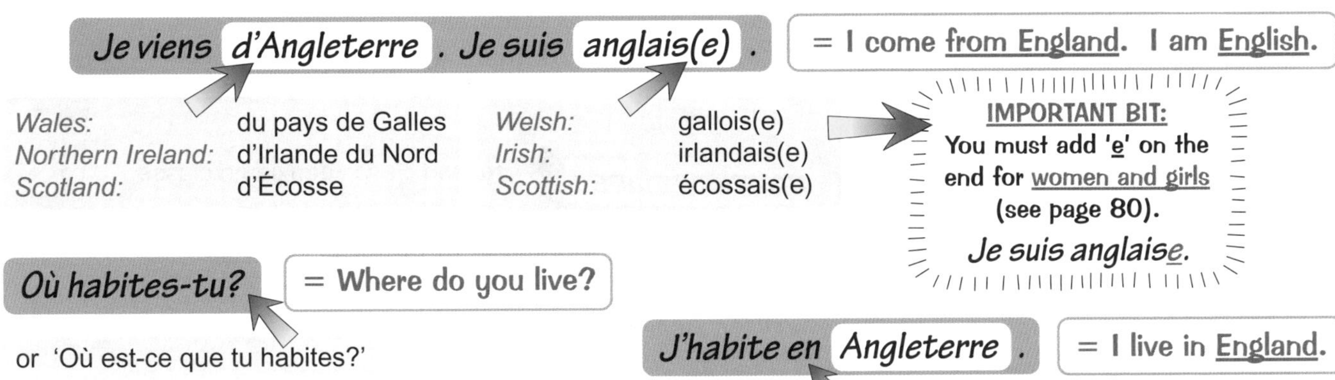

Je viens d'Angleterre. Je suis anglais(e). = I come from England. I am English.

Wales:	du pays de Galles	*Welsh:*	gallois(e)
Northern Ireland:	d'Irlande du Nord	*Irish:*	irlandais(e)
Scotland:	d'Écosse	*Scottish:*	écossais(e)

IMPORTANT BIT: You must add 'e' on the end for women and girls (see page 80).
Je suis anglaise.

Où habites-tu? = Where do you live?

or 'Où est-ce que tu habites?'

J'habite en Angleterre. = I live in England.

Use 'en' for feminine countries and masculine ones beginning with a vowel, and 'au' for all other masculine countries. For plural countries, it's 'aux'.

Learn these foreign countries

You also need to understand where other people come from.

Algeria:	l'Algérie (fem.)	*African:*	africain(e)
America:	l'Amérique (fem.) / les États-Unis (masc.)	*Algerian:*	algérien(ne)
Australia:	l'Australie (fem.)	*American:*	américain(e)
Belgium:	la Belgique	*Australian:*	australien(ne)
Canada:	le Canada	*Belgian:*	belge
China:	la Chine	*Canadian:*	canadien(ne)
France:	la France	*Chinese:*	chinois(e)
Germany:	l'Allemagne (fem.)	*French:*	français(e)
India:	l'Inde (fem.)	*German:*	allemand(e)
Italy:	l'Italie (fem.)	*Indian:*	indien(ne)
Japan:	le Japon	*Italian:*	italien(ne)
Morocco:	le Maroc	*Japanese:*	japonais(e)
Poland:	la Pologne	*Moroccan:*	marocain(e)
Portugal:	le Portugal	*Polish:*	polonais(e)
Spain:	l'Espagne (fem.)	*Portuguese:*	portugais(e)
Switzerland:	la Suisse	*Spanish:*	espagnol(e)
		Swiss:	suisse

L'Irlande du Nord
L'Écosse
La Grande-Bretagne
La République d'Irlande
L'Angleterre
La Hollande
La Pologne
Le pays de Galles
L'Allemagne
La Belgique
La France
L'Autriche
La Suisse
L'Italie
Le Portugal
L'Espagne

England:	l'Angleterre (f.)
Northern Ireland:	l'Irlande du Nord (f.)
Scotland:	l'Écosse (f.)
Wales:	le pays de Galles
Great Britain:	la Grande-Bretagne
Republic of Ireland:	l'Irlande

IMPORTANT: Don't use a capital letter for all these adjectives.

English:	anglais(e)
Irish:	irlandais(e)
Scottish:	écossais(e)
Welsh:	gallois(e)
British:	britannique

Hidden a gender...

Most of the countries are feminine, but there are a few sneaky exceptions which are masculine. And with the ones where the French word is a bit like the English, check you've got the spelling right. Don't just look at them and assume you know them because they look familiar.

Catching the Train

Trains, planes and automobiles... Well, just trains for now. This page gives you a few of the basics you might come across in the exam. Examiners like this topic — I think they all have shares in rail companies.

Je vais prendre le train — I'm going to take the train

Here's how to buy a ticket. You'd be nuts not to learn this.

Est-ce qu'il y a un train pour Paris ? = Is there a train to Paris?

Un aller simple pour Paris, en première classe. = One single to Paris, first class.

second class: deuxième classe

Two: Deux
Three: Trois

single(s): aller(s) simple(s)
return(s): aller-retour(s)

Un aller-retour pour Paris, s'il vous plaît. = One return ticket to Paris, please.

Vous voyagez quand? — When are you travelling?

Here are a few more details about rail travel.

Je voudrais aller à Caen, samedi. = I would like to travel to Caen on Saturday.

today: aujourd'hui
next Monday: lundi prochain
on the tenth of June: le dix juin

Quand est-ce que le train part pour Caen? = When does the train leave for Caen ?

arrive at: arrive à

Le train part de quel quai? = Which platform does the train leave from?

For more info on times and dates, see page 2.

And this is how to ask where stuff is.

Où est le quai, s'il vous plaît? = Where is the platform, please?

the waiting room: la salle d'attente
the left luggage: la consigne

Où sont les toilettes, s'il vous plaît? = Where are the toilets, please?

the ticket office: les guichets (masc.)

What's French for 'Not ANOTHER strike'...

Ah yes, the French love their trains, but even more than that they love leaving their trains to rest while they go off and wave a placard in the air. Anyway, assume the trains will be running during your next visit to the continent, and learn all this wonderful vocabulary in anticipation.

Catching the Train

You'll need to know a bit about the French rail network too. You won't believe how exciting it is.

Est-ce que tu prends l'Eurostar? — Do you take the Eurostar?

Eurostar... don't you just love it...

Je prends l'Eurostar de St Pancras à la gare du Nord à Paris.

= I take the Eurostar from St Pancras to the gare du Nord in Paris.

Le voyage dure deux heures et demie. = The journey lasts two and a half hours.

C'est plus pratique que l'avion. = It's more practical than the plane.

more expensive:	plus cher
quicker:	plus vite

See page 84 for comparing things.

Je préfère prendre le bateau. = I prefer to take the ferry.

Le chemin de fer — The railway

There are a few different types of trains and stations in France, and you'll need to know them.

La SNCF — Société Nationale des Chemins de fer Français — wow, no wonder they shortened it. This is the normal French train network. A train station in French is une gare SNCF.

Le TGV — Train à Grande Vitesse — the pride of the French railway system, these provide high-speed links between big cities.

Not a TGV

Le Métro — Métropolitain — the underground. A tube station is une station de métro (not une gare...).

You might have to listen to a Railway Announcement...

Le train pour Bordeaux part du quai numéro huit à quinze heures quarante-cinq.

= The train to Bordeaux leaves from platform 8 at 15:45.

And to finish, more vocab... Yes, it's as dull as a big dull thing, but it's also vital.

to depart:	partir	*to get on:*	monter dans
departure:	le départ	*to get off:*	descendre de
to arrive:	arriver	*timetable:*	l'horaire (masc.)
arrival:	l'arrivée (fem.)	*composter le billet:*	to punch the ticket

I would catch the train — but it's a bit heavy...*

Lucky you... examiners love to ask about travelling. So you'd better make sure you can answer all the questions they could throw at you about it. The thing is, even if you find this really boring now, when it gets to the exam, you'll be wishing you'd bothered. No doubt about that.

* The writer responsible for this feeble joke has now fled the country.

All Kinds of Transport

Here's what you need to know about other forms of transport. This is another one of those topics that you'll need to know really well — and you need to know loads of vocab for it, too.

Comment vas-tu aux magasins? — How do you get to the shops?

You might need to say how you get about:

Je vais aux magasins à pied. = I go to the shops on foot.

D'habitude, je vais en ville en bus. = I normally go into town by bus.

to school: à l'école / au collège

Je vais chez mes grands-parents par le train. = I go to my grandparents' house by train.

by bus:	en bus / en autobus
on the underground:	en métro
by car:	en voiture
by coach:	en car / en autocar
by boat:	en bateau
by plane:	en avion
by Eurostar:	en Eurostar
by bike:	à vélo
by motorbike:	à moto

Le départ et l'arrivée — Departure and arrival

These are the kinds of questions which could come up when travelling. Or in your exam, perhaps.

Est-ce qu'il y a un bus pour Toulouse? = Is there a bus to Toulouse?

a flight: un vol *a coach:* un car *a train:* un train

Quand part le prochain bus pour Amiens? = When does the next bus to Amiens leave?

the (next) coach: le (prochain) car *the (next) flight:* le (prochain) vol

Quand est-ce que l'avion arrive à Marseille? = When does the plane arrive in Marseilles?

Quel bus...? — Which bus...?

No doubt about it — you need to be able to ask which bus or train goes where. Just learn this.

Quel bus va au centre-ville, s'il vous plaît? = Which bus goes to the town centre, please?

Which train... : Quel train...

to the station:	à la gare
to the airport:	à l'aéroport (masc.)
to the bus station:	à la gare routière

Buses? I can take them or leave them...

A doddle. Well, it will be if you bother to learn it now. There's a chance it'll come up in your speaking assessments, so practise saying it out loud until there's not a bus driver in France who could catch you out. Shouldn't be too tough, really. "I'm going..." is "Je vais..." and that's that.

Planning Your Holiday

Money transactions, excursions and hiring stuff... all extremely important aspects of effective holiday planning. If you want to get great marks, you'd better get learning these unbelievably useful phrases.

Le bureau de change — The currency exchange

Well, you won't get far without money, will you — so learn it well.

Je voudrais changer de l'argent . = I would like to change some money.

£50: cinquante livres sterling

Je voudrais cinq cents euros , s'il vous plaît. = I'd like 500 euros, please.

Voulez-vous voir une pièce d'identité ? = Do you want to see proof of identity?

Le syndicat d'initiative — The tourist office

Here's how you find out what a town's got to offer...

Pouvez-vous me donner des renseignements sur le zoo , s'il vous plaît?

= Can you give me information about the zoo, please?

the town: la ville

Quelles sont les excursions? — What are the excursions?

Est-ce qu'il y a des excursions autour de Lyon ?

any museums in Metz: des musées à Metz

= Are there any excursions around Lyons?

Je voudrais visiter Versailles . = I'd like to visit Versailles.

to go to a museum: aller au musée
to visit the castle: visiter le château

from the church: de l'église (fem.)
from the market: du marché

Le car part de l'hôtel de ville à une heure et demie . = The coach leaves from the town hall at half past one.

The train: Le train
2 o'clock: deux heures
3:15: trois heures quinze

La location de vélos — Bike hire

Je voudrais louer un vélo pour deux jours .

one week: une semaine

a car: une voiture

= I'd like to hire a bike for two days.

Higher...higher...

Tourists? Initiative? Who are they kidding...

Everyone knows tourists just blindly follow the person at the front holding the umbrella, so why call the tourist office a syndicat d'initiative... I dunno, but I bet it's a word you won't forget now...

Holiday Accommodation

This page has all the words you need to know about hotels, hostels, camping and foreign exchanges. It's really useful stuff, so you'd better get learning...

Je cherche un logement — I'm looking for somewhere to stay

Learn these different places to stay...

hotel: l'hôtel (masc.)

youth hostel: l'auberge de jeunesse (fem.)

campsite: le camping

self-catering cottage: le gîte

Learn this vocabulary for Hotels and Hostels

VERBS USED IN HOTELS:

to recommend:	recommander	*to stay:*	rester
to reserve:	réserver	*to leave:*	partir
to confirm:	confirmer	*to cost:*	coûter

THINGS YOU MIGHT WANT TO ASK FOR:

full board (room + all meals):	la pension complète
half board (room + some meals):	la demi-pension

PARTS OF A HOTEL OR YOUTH HOSTEL:

restaurant:	le restaurant
dining room:	la salle à manger
dormitory:	le dortoir
lift:	l'ascenseur (masc.)
stairs:	l'escalier (masc.)
car park:	le parking

THINGS ABOUT YOUR ROOM:

key:	la clé
balcony:	le balcon
bath:	le bain
shower:	la douche
washbasin:	le lavabo

PAYING FOR YOUR STAY:

bill:	la note
(set) price:	le prix (fixe)

Je fais un échange — I'm going on a school exchange

If you get a question about exchange visits, don't panic. Chances are the vocab will be very similar to the stuff you've learnt for other types of holiday.

Je reste chez une famille française. = I'm staying with a French family.

with my penfriend: chez mon correspondant / ma correspondante

C'est bien de parler français tous les jours. = It's good to speak French every day.

see how the French live: voir comment vivent les français

Pension? — but I'm only sixteen...

If anything on logements comes up, you'll be glad I put this page in. It might look like another load of vocabulary, but it's your ticket to a decent mark. If you learn it all, you'll sail through this topic.

Booking a Room / Pitch

It's crucial when you're planning a holiday to be able to talk about your preference for a suite with a gold-plated bath and a view of the Eiffel Tower. Learn this page and you'll be laughing.

Avez-vous des chambres libres? — Do you have any rooms free?

Je voudrais une chambre *pour une personne*. = I'd like a single room.

You could be a bit more specific and use these.

room with a bath: chambre avec bain
room with a balcony: chambre avec balcon

double: pour deux personnes

For more numbers, see page 1.

Je voudrais rester ici deux nuits. = I'd like to stay here two nights.

for one night: une nuit

C'est combien par nuit pour une personne? = How much is it per night for one person?

If there's more than one person, use deux personnes, trois personnes etc.

D'accord, on prend la chambre. = OK, we'll take the room.

Désolé(e), c'est trop cher. = Sorry, it's too expensive.

Au camping — At the campsite

Even if you're not the outdoorsy type it's a good idea to get familiar with this camping vocab for your exams.

Je voudrais un emplacement *pour* une nuit. = I'd like a pitch for one night.

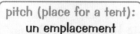

two weeks: deux semaines

pitch (place for a tent): un emplacement

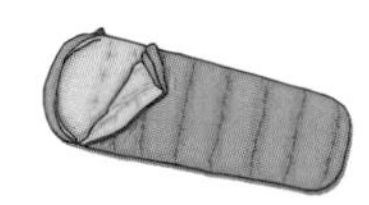

sleeping bag: un sac de couchage

caravan: une caravane

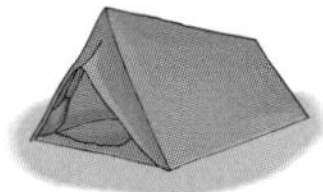

tent: une tente

You may have to book ahead. See page 11 on writing formal letters.

YOU MIGHT NEED THESE PHRASES TOO:

Is there drinking water here?:	Est-ce qu'il y a de l'eau potable ici?
Can I make a fire here?:	Est-ce que je peux faire du feu ici?
Where can I find...?:	Où est-ce que je peux trouver... ?

Tired arms — well, you try pitching for a whole night...

Even if you're never going to go on holiday to France, get this page learnt. Make sure you know all the example sentences, and the extra vocab you can stick into each one. It's the only way.

Where / When is...?

Here's how French people ask <u>where</u> and <u>when things are</u>. It's all pretty important stuff for you to know...

Ask where things are — use 'Où est... ?'

Knowing how the French ask <u>where</u> things are is supremely important — get these <u>learnt</u>.

Où est le restaurant, s'il vous plaît? = Where is <u>the restaurant</u>, please?

the car park:	le parking
the telephone:	le téléphone

See page 46 for more places you might need to find.

Où sont les toilettes ? = Where are <u>the toilets?</u>

If the place you're looking for is plural (e.g. has 'les' in front of it), remember to use 'Où sont...' instead of 'Où est...'

Use 'Elle' for 'la' words, 'Elles' or 'Ils' for plural words and 'Il' for 'le' words.

Use 'au' here because 'étage' is masculine. Use 'à la' for feminine words, e.g. 'elle est à la piscine'.

Elle est au troisième étage. = <u>It's</u> on the <u>third floor</u>.

fourth floor:	quatrième étage
second floor:	deuxième étage
first floor:	premier étage
ground floor:	rez-de-chaussée

C'est un "stick-up". Où est le "money"?

For higher floor numbers, see page 1.

OTHER WORDS YOU MIGHT NEED:

straight on:	tout droit	*on the left*	à gauche
upstairs:	en haut	*on the right:*	à droite
downstairs:	en bas	*at the end of the corridor:*	au bout du couloir

À quelle heure... ? — What time... ?

When you've understood <u>where</u> everything is, you'll need to know <u>when</u> things happen, too...

Le petit déjeuner est à quelle heure, s'il vous plaît? = What time is <u>breakfast</u>, please?

lunch:	le déjeuner
evening meal:	le dîner

For more times, see page 2.

Il est servi entre six heures et huit heures. = It's served between six and eight o'clock.

You've lost me...

A really <u>easy</u> page this — just <u>two key questions</u> and a few responses to learn. Make sure you do learn it though, because this is exactly the sort of material that's been cropping up in French listening tests since the beginning of time. And one day you might need to <u>find the loo</u>, too...

Problems with Accommodation

Accommodation with problems... cockroaches in the bath, rats in the kitchens — that kind of thing. Like revision, it's not pleasant, but you know the drill — somebody's got to deal with it...

Il y a un problème... — There's a problem...

Make sure you can write about at least two problems — safety in numbers.

Il n'y a pas de serviettes dans la chambre. = There aren't any towels in the room.

glasses: verres (masc.)

Il fait trop chaud. = It's too hot.

cold: froid

La télévision est cassée. = The TV is broken.

The chair: La chaise

'Cassée' has two 'e's because 'télévision' is feminine. If it was describing a masculine word it would only have one. See page 80.

La douche ne marche pas. = The shower doesn't work.

The phone: Le téléphone

Je ne suis pas content(e) — I'm not happy

Il y a de l'eau partout. = There is water everywhere.

sand: du sable

La chambre est trop petite. = The room is too small.

The bathroom: La salle de bains

'Petite' has an 'e' on the end because 'chambre' is feminine. See page 80.

Il y a trop de bruit — je ne peux pas dormir. = There is too much noise — I can't sleep.

Est-ce que vous pouvez faire quelque chose? — Can you do something?

Est-ce que nous pouvons avoir plus de serviettes ? = Can we have more towels?

soap: savon (masc.)

J'ai besoin d'un lit de plus. = I need one more bed.

key: une clé

Je voudrais une autre chambre. = I would like another room.

'There's water everywhere' — 'Well, this is a cruise, Sir...'

Fingers crossed, whether you're in a B&B in Calais or a 5-star hotel in Paris, you'll never need to complain about this stuff when you're on holiday in France. But learn this page just in case.

At a Restaurant

If you've been to France, a lot of these signs and phrases could be familiar to you. The restaurant theme tends to crop up in the exams year after year, after year, after year, after... — so this is important stuff.

Au restaurant... — In the restaurant...

Here are some words and phrases you'll find useful when talking about restaurants.

= Open

= Dish of the day
Specialities

Attendez ici s'il vous plaît

= Wait here, please

Heures d'ouverture

= Opening hours

Fermé

= Closed

Service compris

= Service included

Défense de fumer

= No smoking

À la carte:
= Individually priced items
Menu à prix fixe:
= Fixed price menu

Pourboire

= Tip

Est-ce que vous avez une table libre? — Do you have a table free?

This part's easy — definitely worth learning.

Je voudrais réserver une table pour quatre *personnes, s'il vous plaît.*

two: deux *three:* trois

= I would like to reserve a table for four, please.

Je voudrais m'asseoir sur la terrasse.

= I'd like to sit on the terrace.

Est-ce que je peux avoir la carte, s'il vous plaît?

= May I have the menu, please?

Où sont *les toilettes, s'il vous plaît?*

is: est *the phone:* le téléphone

= Where are the toilets, please?

See page 48 for help asking where things are.

I have a dream today, that all tables shall be free...

When a restaurant bit comes up in the exam you'll be kicking yourself if you haven't revised it. Learn all of it, and you'll really impress. No missing bits out — if you learn all the stuff on this page (and all the other pages), it'll all be OK. And you'll be able to get fed in France. Bonus.

At a Restaurant

Now it's time for that all-important part... opinions. You'll need to talk about the foods you prefer and know how to state any problems you have with a meal. Revise this and your French will be complete. Almost.

Je voudrais... — I would like...

See page 13 for food vocab.

starter: hors d'œuvre *(masc.)* *dessert:* dessert (masc.)

Comme plat principal, je voudrais la pizza au poulet.

the steak: le bifteck *the chocolate cake:* le gâteau au chocolat

= For main course, I'd like the chicken pizza.

Désolé, il n'y a plus de porc — Sorry, there's no more pork

You may need to understand changes if they haven't got your order or if a mistake is made.

Je vais prendre l'agneau à la place du porc. = I'll have the lamb instead of the pork.

the lamb: l'agneau *the pork:* le porc

Il y a une erreur. Je n'ai pas commandé le poisson. = There's been a mistake. I didn't order the fish.

Mon repas n'est pas bon — My meal isn't good

The pork: Le porc
The coffee: Le café

Le bœuf est froid. *is too hot:* est trop chaud

= The beef is cold.

J'ai trouvé un cheveu dans ma soupe. = I found a hair in my soup.

a mouse: une souris

On attend depuis une heure. = We've been waiting for an hour.

Est-ce que vous avez fini? — Have you finished?

There's no getting away from having to know this. You can't leave without paying.

Est-ce que je peux payer? = May I pay?

L'addition, s'il vous plaît. = The bill, please.

Est-ce que le service est compris? = Is service included?

Thanks Mr Federer, the service was ace...

Restaurants — fun to eat at, but a bit of a mouthful when it comes to GCSE French revision. Two pages that will be supremely useful in the exam once you've mastered 'em — so go for it...

Talking About Your Holiday

Everyone wants to bore people by telling them all about their holidays. By the time you've finished this page you'll be able to bore people in French... and get good marks.

Où es-tu allé(e)? — Where did you go?

This is where you went: ...and this is when you went:

Je suis allé(e) aux États-Unis , il y a deux semaines .

= I went to the USA, two weeks ago.

to Spain: en Espagne
to France: en France
to Ireland: en Irlande

a week ago: il y a une semaine
last month: le mois dernier
in July: en juillet
in the summer: en été

Other dates and times: pages 2–3.
A bigger list of countries: page 41.

Avec qui étais-tu en vacances? — Who were you on holiday with?

You'd better answer this question, otherwise there'll be all sorts of gossip.

J'étais en vacances avec ma famille pendant un mois .

= I was on holiday with my family for a month.

a fortnight: quinze jours
two weeks: deux semaines

my brother: mon frère
my friends: mes ami(e)s
my class: ma classe

For the imperfect tense, see page 98.
For more on family, see page 18.

Qu'est-ce que tu as fait? — What did you do?

You need to be able to say what you did on holiday — learn it well.

Je suis allé(e) à la plage .

= I went to the beach.

to the disco: en discothèque *to the museum:* au musée

For other places, see page 57.

For other sports and activities, see page 26.

This is a reflexive verb — see page 99 for more on these.

Je me suis amusé(e) .

= I had fun.

I swam in the sea: Je me suis baigné(e) dans la mer
I played tennis: J'ai joué au tennis

Comment as-tu voyagé? — How did you travel?

And, leaving the best til last, the journey...

Nous avons voyagé en voiture .

= We travelled by car.

by plane: en avion
by boat: en bateau
by train: par le train / en train
by bike: à vélo

For more types of transport, see page 44.

So, celeb Z-list — what's the jungle really like...

One final useful tip before you move on — you don't have to talk about a real holiday. You might find it easier to make one up using countries and things you find easy to remember and/or say...

Talking About Your Holiday

Opinions and tales of woe — the examiners love them. So plough on and learn this stuff as well...

Comment était le voyage? — How was the trip?

Comment étaient tes vacances? = How was your holiday?

Elles étaient bons. = It was good.

Les vacances étaient formidables. = The holiday was great.

Elles n'étaient pas bonnes. = It wasn't good.

Comme ci comme ça. = So-so.

Quelle catastrophe — What a disaster

Sometimes things don't quite go to plan when you're on holiday.

Limb-breakers.

Nous avons fait du ski. Ma sœur s'est cassé la jambe.

= We went skiing. My sister broke her leg.

her arm: le bras
her nose: le nez

her ticket: son billet *her suitcase:* sa valise

Ma mère a oublié son passeport. Elle n'a pas pu prendre l'avion.

= My mum forgot her passport. She couldn't get on the plane.

J'étais malade et j'ai perdu mon sac à main. = I was ill and I lost my handbag.

my mp3 player: mon lecteur mp3 *my wallet:* mon portefeuille

Mon frère était méchant pendant toute la semaine. = My brother was horrible all week.

Il a plu tous les jours — It rained every day

If they ask you to compare different holidays, the weather's a good place to start...

En Italie, il faisait plus chaud qu'en Écosse. = In Italy it was hotter than in Scotland.

En France, il pleuvait moins qu'en Espagne. = In France, it rained less than in Spain.

This is the comparative. For more examples, see page 84.

For more on weather, see page 55.

The rain in Spain falls mainly whenever I'm there...

Ah, Brits and the weather. We could go to Zanzibar, ride an elephant, feed monkeys and swim with dolphins and we'd still just tell people that it rained more than it did last year in Scunthorpe etc...

Talking About Your Holiday

More on holidays — yay. This time it's about where you're planning on going, or where you'd like to go.

Où vas-tu aller l'année prochaine? — Where will you go next year?

Je vais aller en Allemagne. = I'm going to go to Germany.

For other countries see page 41.

For the future tense, see page 94.

Je n'ai pas encore décidé. = I haven't decided yet.

Comment vas-tu voyager? = How are you going to travel?

Je vais voyager par le train. = I'm going to travel by train.

Qu'est-ce que tu vas prendre? = What are you going to take?

Je vais prendre des livres et mon maillot de bain. = I'm going to take some books and my swimsuit.

Est-ce que les vacances sont importantes? — Do you think holidays are important?

If your speaking assessment's on holidays, you might be asked to give your opinions on holidays in general.

Bien sûr. On ne peut pas travailler tout le temps. = Of course. You can't work all the time.

Non, elles ne sont pas importantes. Je préfère dépenser mon argent sur d'autres choses. = No, they're not important. I prefer spending my money on other things.

Est-ce qu'on prend trop de vacances? = Do we take too many holidays?

Oui, tous ces vols sont mauvais pour l'environnement. = Yes — all these flights are bad for the environment.

trips abroad: voyages à l'étranger

Non, c'est bien de voir d'autres pays. = No. It's good to see other countries.

My opinion's on holiday...

Maybe don't use that one on the day of your speaking assessment — telling your teacher that your point of view is on a short minibreak is unlikely to go down well. Learn to say what you think...

The Weather

You might have to listen to a weather forecast in your listening exam. But don't panic — learn the weather stuff in the present and future tenses given here and you'll be OK. More than OK — stupendous.

Quel temps fait-il? — What's the weather like?

These short sentences are the ones you definitely can't do without — and they're easy.

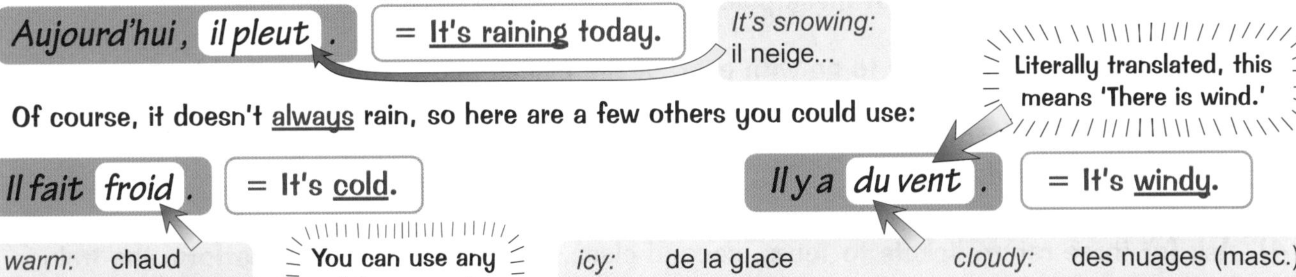

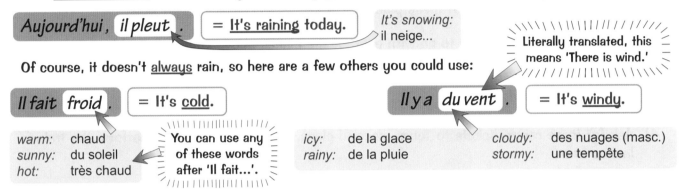

Aujourd'hui, il pleut. = It's raining today.

It's snowing: il neige...

Of course, it doesn't always rain, so here are a few others you could use:

Literally translated, this means 'There is wind.'

Il fait froid. = It's cold.

warm: chaud
sunny: du soleil
hot: très chaud

You can use any of these words after 'Il fait...'.

Il y a du vent. = It's windy.

icy: de la glace
rainy: de la pluie
cloudy: des nuages (masc.)
stormy: une tempête

Quel temps va-t-il faire demain? — What will the weather be like tomorrow?

This is quite easy, and it sounds dead impressive:

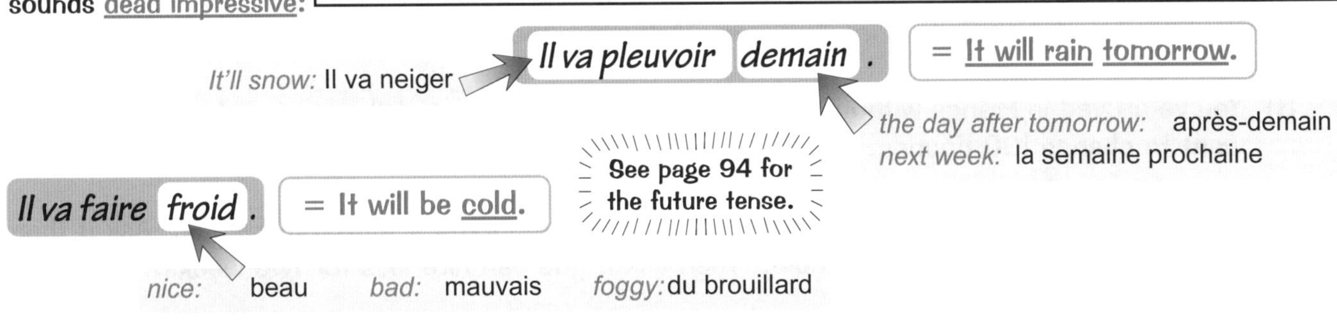

It'll snow: Il va neiger

Il va pleuvoir demain. = It will rain tomorrow.

the day after tomorrow: après-demain
next week: la semaine prochaine

Il va faire froid. = It will be cold.

See page 94 for the future tense.

nice: beau *bad:* mauvais *foggy:* du brouillard

You need to understand a weather forecast

Here's a real weather forecast — time to show what you can do. You won't know all the words, but don't panic. Work through this one — you should be able to get the gist by looking at the words you do know.

La météo d'aujourd'hui
Aujourd'hui il va faire chaud partout en France. Demain il y aura du vent dans le sud et des nuages dans le nord.

Today's Weather Forecast
Today it will be warm everywhere in France. Tomorrow it will be windy in the south and cloudy in the north.

Tomorrow it'll be wet.

in the east: dans l'est *in the west:* dans l'ouest

France — where time is weather...

'Le temps' can either mean 'time' or 'weather', but you should always be able to tell from the context which one it is. Weather's a favourite with examiners, so you need to learn the examples on this page and the bits of vocab — then you'll be fine. (Just like the weather, with any luck...)

Revision Summary

It's that time again folks... another dreaded revision summary. Don't dread it. Work in harmony with it, so that by the time you've answered all of these questions (several times), you'll feel like you're a fully-fledged Frenchified person, one who is fully able to take on that exam. OK, cut the 'yoga speak' — just practise these questions till you can answer them in your sleep.

1) Write down four countries in the UK and five other countries, in French. How would you say that you came from each of these places?
2) Write down the nationality to go with each of the places above (but in French).
3) You're at a French train station. How would you say, in French, that you'd like to travel to Marseilles on Sunday?
4) Ask for three return tickets to Tours, second class. Ask when and what platform the train leaves from.
5) How do you say these in French?
   a) the waiting room b) the timetable c) the ticket counter d) the departure
6) Say that you go to school by car, but to town on foot.
7) You've missed the bus to Pont-Audemer. Ask when the next bus leaves and when it'll arrive.
8) You've arrived in France without any euros. Tell the assistant at the bureau de change that you want to change 100 pounds.
9) Imagine that you are a first class impersonator. Impersonate a tourist in France. Ask if there are any excursions around Grenoble. Then ask if you can hire skis for two weeks.
10) What are these in French? a) hotel b) youth hostel c) campsite d) cottage
11) How do you say these in French? a) key b) bill c) stairs d) tent e) sleeping bag
12) Your friend announces: 'Je reste chez une famille française et je parle français tous les jours.' What have they just told you about the school exchange they're on?
13) You arrive at a French hotel. Say you want one double room with a balcony for five nights.
14) Ask where the restaurant is, and what time breakfast is, out loud and in French.
15) You've just arrived at a grotty French hotel. It's too hot and the shower doesn't work. What would you say to the lady at reception?
16) You're in a restaurant. It's all gone wrong — you want to complain. The lamb is cold and there's a hair in your soup. How would you say all this in French?
17) Think about your last holiday. Say where you went, how you got there and who you went with. Then tell us about two things that happened while you were there.
18) Are holidays important? Give at least one reason why or why not.
19) You've just listened to the weather forecast. Say that tomorrow it will be hot.

Names of Buildings

If you're going to talk about your town, you need to know the names for buildings.
Yes, it's a bit dull, but you absolutely have to learn them.

Learn all these bâtiments — buildings

These are the basic, bog-standard 'learn-them-or-else' buildings. (Building = le bâtiment.)

the bank: la banque

the butcher's: la boucherie

the church: l'église (fem.)

the theatre: le théâtre

the railway station: la gare

the market: le marché

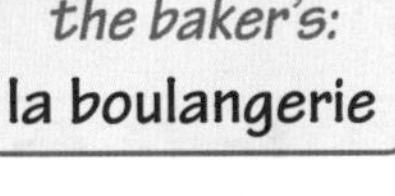

the baker's: la boulangerie

the cinema: le cinéma

the supermarket: le supermarché

the castle: le château

the post office: la poste

the library: la bibliothèque

D'autres lieux — Other places

OK, I'll come clean. There are absolutely loads of buildings you need to know. Here's the rest:

See page 33 for more shops.

SOME SHOPS

shop:	le magasin
bookshop:	la librairie
newsagent:	le tabac
chemist's:	la pharmacie
cake shop:	la pâtisserie

TOURISTY BITS

hotel:	l'hôtel (masc.)
youth hostel:	l'auberge de jeunesse (fem.)
travel agent:	l'agence de voyages (fem.)
tourist information office:	le syndicat d'initiative
museum:	le musée

OTHER IMPORTANT PLACES

cathedral:	la cathédrale	*bus station:*	la gare routière
park:	le parc	*town hall:*	l'hôtel de ville (masc.), la mairie
swimming pool:	la piscine	*sports ground:*	le terrain de sport
airport:	l'aéroport (masc.)	*recycling centre:*	le centre de recyclage
stadium:	le stade	*police station:*	le commissariat
town centre:	le centre-ville	*university:*	l'université (fem.)
hospital:	l'hôpital (masc.)	*school:*	le collège, l'école (fem.)

Take a butcher's... (and a baker's... and a candlesti...)

Learning vocab is just such great fun, don't you think... OK, so it's pretty dull. But it will come up in the exams. The best way to learn it is to turn over the page and try to write all the words down. Then look back and have another go at the ones you got wrong. It's boring, but it works.

Asking Directions

It's pretty likely you'll get at least one question about asking or understanding directions. If you don't learn this stuff, that's one question you won't be able to answer. That's a good enough reason to learn it.

Où est... ? — Where is... ?

Asking where something is is dead easy — 'Où est...' plus the place name:

See page 57 for more buildings.

Où est la poste, s'il vous plaît? = Where is the post office, please?

Est-ce qu'il y a une bibliothèque près d'ici? = Is there a library near here?

Le cinéma est... — The cinema is...

Le cinéma est entre la banque et le parc. = The cinema is between the bank and the park.

here / there:	ici / là-bas	*behind the bank:*	derrière la banque	*opposite the bank:*	en face de la banque
next to the park:	à côté du parc	*on the corner:*	au coin	*in front of the school:*	devant l'école

C'est loin d'ici? — Is it far from here?

It's a good idea to check distance, before letting yourself in for a 3-hour trek:

Est-ce que le cinéma est loin d'ici? = Is the cinema far from here?

the post office: la poste
the park: le parc

C'est à deux kilomètres d'ici. = It's two kilometres from here.

several kilometres: à quelques kilomètres   *far:* loin   *near:* près

Use 'pour aller à...?' to ask the way

You'll probably hear people asking directions in your listening test.

Library
So, tell me again how to get to the library.

(to a woman): madame   *to the castle:* au château   *to the hospital:* à l'hôpital

Pardon monsieur, pour aller à la banque, s'il vous plaît? = Excuse me sir, how do I get to the bank, please?

Use 'au' for 'le' words, 'à la' for 'la' words, and 'à l'' for words starting with a vowel and most words which start with an 'h'. See page 79.

Look at page 1 for more stuff on 1st, 2nd, etc.

LEARN THIS IMPORTANT VOCAB FOR DIRECTIONS

go straight on:	allez tout droit	*go / turn right at the traffic lights:*	tournez à droite aux feux rouges
go right:	tournez à droite	*go straight on, past the church:*	allez tout droit, devant l'église
go left:	tournez à gauche	*take the first road on the left:*	prenez la première rue à gauche

How do you get to Wembley — years of practice...

Cover it up, scribble it down, check what you got wrong, and try it again. That's the way to learn this stuff. Keep at it until you know it all — then you'll be really ready for the exam. Just reading the page is nowhere near enough — you wouldn't remember it tomorrow, never mind in the exam.

Where You're From

This page deals with regions and cities that you'll be expected to know the name of in French. Don't just worry about where you come from — you might come across these in any part of the assessments.

Tu es de quelle région? — Which region are you from?

You'll definitely need to recognise lots of regions of France and French-speaking places:

Je viens de la Bretagne. = I come from Brittany.

Remember that 'de + le = du'. See page 79.

from the centre of France:	du Massif Central
from Corsica:	de la Corse
from the south of France:	du Midi

The counties of Britain have a 'le' or a 'du' in front of them.

J'habite dans le Surrey. = I live in Surrey.

Je viens du Surrey. = I come from Surrey.

Les grandes villes — Cities

Normally the names of cities are the same in French and English, but there are a few exceptions you're expected to know.

Dover:	Douvres
Edinburgh:	Édimbourg
London:	Londres

J'habite au bord de la mer — I live by the sea

There are a few names of seas and mountains you need to know.

the Atlantic:	l'Atlantique (masc.)	*the mountain(s):*	la montagne
the Mediterranean:	la Méditerranée	*the Pyrenees:*	les Pyrénées (fem.)
the English Channel:	la Manche	*the Alps:*	les Alpes (fem.)

Mon village se trouve au pied des Pyrénées. = My village lies at the foot of the Pyrenees.

You might need to say you live near a river:

Une rivière = A river

J'habite dans une ville située sur le Severn. = I live in a town situated on the Severn.

Thames:	la Tamise
Seine:	la Seine
Rhone:	le Rhône

Learn ev'ry mountain, search high and low...

Having said that, there's not an awful lot to learn here, but it is the kind of stuff that can catch you out if you haven't seen it before. Have another quick look at this page before you turn over.

Talking About Where You Live

You'll have to understand and answer questions about where you live.
If you've learnt this, you'll be able to understand and answer. Simple as that.

Où est-ce que tu habites? — Where do you live?

You won't get through GCSE French without needing this vocab — so make sure you learn it well.

J'habite à Barrow. = I live in Barrow.

Barrow se trouve dans le nord-ouest de l'Angleterre. = Barrow's in the north-west of England.

See page 41 for more countries.

the north: le nord
the south: le sud
the west: l'ouest (masc.)
the east: l'est (masc.)

You have to write about life 'dans ta ville' — 'in your town'

Practise writing a description of your town or your favourite town — know this vocab well...

Qu'est-ce qu'il y a dans ta ville? = What is there in your town?

Il y a un marché. = There's a market.

See page 57 for more buildings and places.

Est-ce que tu aimes vivre à Barrow? = Do you like living in Barrow?

J'aime vivre à Barrow. = I like living in Barrow.

I don't like: Je n'aime pas

Que penses-tu de Barrow? — What do you think of Barrow?

Descriptions of towns could come up in any of your assessments — it's need-to-know stuff.

La ville est très intéressante. = The town is very interesting.

boring: ennuyeuse
great: chouette
dirty: sale
clean: propre
quiet: tranquille

Il y a beaucoup à faire. = There's lots to do.

enough: assez
always something: toujours quelque chose

Il n'y a rien à faire. = There's nothing to do.

There's more about where you live on the next page.

Lie if you need to, but make it believable.

Longer descriptions may seem tough at first — they're simply all the bits you already know put together...

J'aime vivre à Barrow, parce qu'il y a toujours quelque chose à faire. = I like living in Barrow, because there's always something to do.

Je n'aime pas vivre à Bogville, parce qu'il n'y a rien à faire. = I don't like living in Bogville, because there's nothing to do.

Barrow — it's wheely great...

If you're from a dreary place with nothing going on, you can make things up (within reason) — chances are there'll be something to say about a place near you. Start with where it is and see how much you can write about it without looking at the page.

Talking About Where You Live

This page isn't too bad — even the tricky stuff is really just a case of 'learn the sentences and learn what words you can change around in them'. If you spend the time on it, it'll become super easy.

Comment est ta ville? — What's your town like?

Lancaster est une grande ville. = Lancaster is a city.

a town: une ville *a village:* un village

Lancaster a quarante-six mille habitants et beaucoup d'industrie. = Lancaster has 46 000 inhabitants and a lot of industry.

Extra marks for style

J'habite au numéro six, rue Armadillo, à Lancaster. = I live at 6, Armadillo Street, Lancaster.

Tu habites avec qui? — Who do you live with?

J'habite avec mes parents. = I live with my parents.

my grandparents: mes grands-parents
my father: mon père *my mother:* ma mère

See p.18 for more people you might live with.

J'aime habiter en famille parce que ... = I like living with family because...

I don't do any housework: je ne fais pas de ménage.
it's very comfortable: c'est très confortable.

Je n'aime pas habiter en famille parce que ... = I don't like living with family because...

my brother annoys me: mon frère m'énerve.
I don't have a private life: je n'ai pas de vie privée.

Chez toi — At your home

Being able to write about where you live and understanding others talking about their home is really important too...

semi-detached house: maison jumelée *detached house:* maison individuelle

J'habite une petite maison moderne. = I live in a small, modern house.

big: grande
pretty: jolie

white: blanche

In French, you don't need 'dans' when you say where you live. Literally you say, 'I live a house'. It's easiest if you think 'habiter' = 'inhabit'.

Mon appartement se trouve près du parc. = My flat is near the park.

the motorway: de l'autoroute (fem.)
the shops: des magasins (masc.)

My house: Ma maison

on the ground floor: au rez-de-chaussée

Mon appartement est au premier étage. = My flat is on the first floor.

Chez — not just for hairdressers...

You need to be able to say where you live — just say "J'habite au numéro..." and then the number of the house or flat, followed by the street name. Easy really. But only if you bother to learn it.

Inside Your Home

You've got to be able to describe your home. Luckily, you don't need to say everything that's in it — just some things. And you can always pretend you don't have that indoor swimming pool...

Comment est ta maison? — What's your house like?

It'll look impressive if you can give more details about your home. Details are the answer...

Il y a six pièces. = There are six rooms.

Comment est la cuisine ? = What's the kitchen like?

Est-ce que la cuisine est grande ? = Is the kitchen big?

the dining room: la salle à manger

comfortable: confortable
nice: joli(e)
great: chouette
beautiful: beau / belle

Le salon est moche. = The living room is ugly.

Est-ce que tu as un jardin? — Have you got a garden?

Il y a un jardin. = There is a garden.

a tree: un arbre
a lawn: une pelouse
a balcony: un balcon
a swimming pool: une piscine

Nous avons des fleurs dans notre jardin. = We have flowers in our garden.

Est-ce que tu as une chambre à toi? — Have you got your own room?

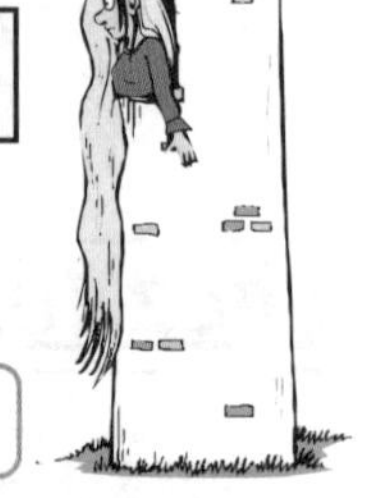

You'll pick up more juicy marks with these...

J'ai une chambre à moi. = I have my own room.

Je partage une chambre avec mon frère. = I share a room with my brother.

Parle-moi de ta chambre... — Tell me about your room

Remember, if these aren't in your room, you can be creative (lie) — get the vocab spot on, though.

Dans ma chambre, il y a ... = In my bedroom there is / there are...

a wardrobe: une armoire *a mirror:* un miroir *a bed:* un lit *some curtains:* des rideaux (masc.)

L'armoire est rouge et les murs sont gris. = The wardrobe is red and the walls are grey.

'L'armoire' is singular, so the verb 'être' is too = est

'Les murs' is plural, so the verb 'être' is too = sont

For once I wish I lived in a one-room bedsit...

It's all about the little details here. Once you've learnt these phrases, you can go into great detail about your Cliff Richard posters and wow everyone with your descriptive abilities. Super.

The Environment

Things get serious when the environment comes up, and you're supposed to have an opinion. It's a chance for you to write or say what you think about something real and important. Go get 'em...

Est-ce que l'environnement est important pour toi?

Is the environment important to you?

Start by introducing your viewpoint...

Oui, je m'intéresse beaucoup à l'environnement.

= Yes, I'm very interested in the environment.

I think the environment is very important: je pense que l'environnement est très important

Non, ça ne m'intéresse pas.

= No, I'm not interested in it.

it doesn't worry me: ça ne m'inquiète pas

Il y a de graves problèmes...

— There are serious problems...

Talk about the problems...

Il y a de la pollution parce qu'il y a trop de circulation.

rubbish: déchets

= There's pollution because there's too much traffic.

dirty: sales

L'air et les rivières sont pollués.

= The air and the rivers are polluted.

Il ne reste pas beaucoup de pétrole.

= There's not much oil left.

Il faut sauver l'environnement

— We must save the environment

And finally the solutions...

On ne doit pas jeter les sacs en plastique.

= We mustn't throw away plastic bags.

cardboard boxes: les boîtes en carton *bottles:* les bouteilles

On doit avoir beaucoup de zones piétonnes.

= We should have lots of pedestrian zones.

public transport: transports en commun *cycle lanes:* pistes cyclables

On peut aussi aller au centre de recyclage.

= We can also go to the recycling centre.

grow vegetables in the garden: cultiver des légumes dans le jardin

Pollution — load of rubbish...

This page is hard — there's loads of vocab, and most of it isn't everyday stuff. Still, just think how much you'll want to kick yourself if it comes up in the exam and you haven't learnt it. Shudder.

Revision Summary

Yippee. I don't really know why I said that. I think I was trying to put a positive spin on a rather rubbish situation... It's another revision summary. You have to do this part to prepare yourself fully for exam time. Do the questions. Get 'em right. Move on with your life. Or do Section Six — it's all about school and jobs and other extremely uplifting topics. Yay.

1) You've arrived in Boulogne and are writing to your penfriend Marie-Claire about the sights. How do you say there's a castle, a swimming pool, a university, a cinema, a cathedral and a theatre?

2) Write down five shops and five other buildings you might find in a town (not the ones above).

3) You need to go to the library. How do you ask where it is, and if it's far away?

4) What do these directions mean: 'La bibliothèque est à un kilomètre d'ici. Tournez à droite, prenez la première rue à gauche et allez tout droit, devant l'église. La bibliothèque est à droite, entre la banque et le cinéma.'

5) A French tourist has come to see your home town and is looking for the youth hostel. Tell him to go straight on, turn left at the traffic lights and the youth hostel is on the corner.

6) Tell your French penfriend Jean-Jacques where you live, whereabouts it is (which country and whether it's in the north or south etc.) and what it's like.

7) Say in French that you like living in your town because there's lots to do.

8) Say your address and describe the place where you live — whether it's a town or a village and how many people live there.

9) Your French friend Marie says: 'J'habite avec mes parents et mon frère. J'aime habiter en famille parce que ma mère fait tout le ménage.' What does she mean?

10) Marie-Françoise lives in a big, modern house. It's near the town centre, shops and a motorway. How would she say this in French?

11) Tom has his own room. It has red walls and a brown wardrobe. It also has a bed, a mirror, and some curtains. How will he say all this in French?

12) Give one reason (in French) why the environment is or isn't important to you.

13) Sofie's worried about global warming. In French, give another example of a problem facing the environment.

14) There's no stopping Sofie — she's just told you she'd like to live in a remote wooden hut and be at one with nature. Suggest some more realistic options for saving the environment. You'll need to mention at least three — she's very set on the wooden hut idea.

School Subjects

There's no way to avoid school and jobs, however much they stress you out. Learn this well — stress less.

Tu fais quelles matières? — What subjects do you do?

Go over these subjects until you know them all really well...

SCIENCES

science:	les sciences (fem.)
physics:	la physique
chemistry:	la chimie
biology:	la biologie

NUMBERS AND STUFF

maths:	les maths (fem.)
IT:	l'informatique (fem.)

ARTS AND CRAFTS

art:	le dessin
music:	la musique
D&T:	les travaux manuels

PHYSICAL EDUCATION

P.E.: l'éducation physique (fem.) / le sport / l'EPS (fem.)

LANGUAGES

French:	le français
German:	l'allemand (masc.)
Spanish:	l'espagnol (masc.)
Italian:	l'italien (masc.)
English:	l'anglais (masc.)

HUMANITIES

history:	l'histoire (fem.)
geography:	la géographie

I study: J'étudie

J'apprends le français. = I'm learning French.

Quelle est ta matière préférée? — What's your favourite subject?

OK, school stuff may not be exciting, but you definitely need to know it.

I don't like: Je n'aime pas
I hate: Je déteste

J'aime les maths. = I like maths.

There's more on how to say what you like and don't like on pages 7–8.

Je préfère la biologie. = I prefer biology.

You can put any school subject in the white boxes.

Ma matière préférée est le sport. = PE is my favourite subject.

Depuis quand...? — How long...?

This isn't here because I like it. It's here because it could be in your assessments. So learn it.

Depuis quand apprends-tu le français? = How long have you been learning French?

Be careful to use the present tense — you don't say 'I have been' as in English. See pages 92-93.

For more on numbers, see page 1.

J'apprends le français depuis trois ans. = I've been learning French for three years.

Midget "j'aime"s — my favourite sweets...

Play around with this page until you've got it firmly lodged in your brain. Make sure you know all the subjects you do really well, and understand the ones you don't do when you see or hear them.

The School Routine

Not the most exciting of pages ever, but it's worth all the effort when you get tricky questions on school routine. Go for short snappy sentences — that way, they're easier to remember.

Comment vas-tu au collège? — How do you get to school?

This bit's basic — know the basics...

by bus: en bus *by bike:* à vélo

Je vais au collège en voiture. = I go to school by car.

Je vais au collège à pied. = I go to school on foot.

Use 'à l'école' or 'au collège' for 'to school'. For more on forms of transport, see page 44.

L'horaire — The timetable

You're right, this timetable is a bit much.

It's important you know how to describe a school day — une journée scolaire.

finish: finissent

Les cours commencent à neuf heures. = Lessons begin at 9.00.

For more on times, see page 2.

Nous avons huit cours par jour. = We have 8 lessons per day.

Chaque cours dure trente minutes. = Each lesson lasts 30 minutes.

Nous faisons une heure de devoirs par jour. = We do one hour of homework a day.

Lunch break: La pause déjeuner

La récréation est à onze heures. = Break is at 11.00.

I talk with friends: Je parle avec mes ami(e)s
I do my homework: Je fais mes devoirs
I play football: Je joue au football

Je mange un fruit dans la cour pendant la récré. = I eat a piece of fruit in the playground at break time.

L'année scolaire — The school year

This is all a bit more tricky but stick with it and you'll get there.

Il y a trois trimestres. = There are three terms.

Nous avons six semaines de vacances en été. = We have six weeks' holiday in the summer.

eight weeks: huit semaines *five days:* cinq jours *at Christmas:* à Noël *at Easter:* à Pâques

J'aime la rentrée parce que ... = I like the start of the new school year because...

I hate: Je déteste

it's good to see my friends: c'est bien de voir mes ami(e)s.
it's boring at home: c'est ennuyeux à la maison.
I don't like studying: je n'aime pas étudier.

I hate my timetable — it's horair-ble...

Don't forget the phrases for your exciting school routine, and the sentences for saying how you go to school. Remember the handy phrase 'par jour' — you can stick it in loads of sentences.

More School Stuff

OK, I know this school stuff is a bit close to home and it's a bit boring. (Well, properly boring actually.) But it's revision — it's unlikely to ever get really good. Power through and you'll reap exam rewards galore.

Portez-vous un uniforme? — Do you wear a uniform?

You may have to understand others talking about the differences between schools in the UK and in France...

Les élèves anglais portent un uniforme à l'école. = English students wear a uniform to school.

See page 35 for more on clothes and colours.

Notre uniforme est un pull rouge, un pantalon gris, une chemise blanche et une cravate verte. = Our uniform is a red jumper, grey trousers, a white shirt and a green tie.

we go to secondary school from the age of 11 to 15:	on va au collège de l'âge d'onze à quinze ans
we study for the 'baccalauréat' at a 'lycée':	on étudie pour le bac au lycée
we go to school on Saturday mornings:	on va au collège le samedi matin.

En France, on ne va pas au collège le mercredi après-midi.

= In France, we don't go to school on a Wednesday afternoon.

Il y a beaucoup de règles — There are lots of rules

On n'a pas le droit de parler dans les couloirs. = We're not allowed to talk in the corridors.

write on the (interactive) whiteboard: écrire sur le tableau blanc (intéractif)
eat in the lab: manger au laboratoire

"Passer un examen" means "to take an exam" rather than to pass one.

En France, on doit passer un examen à quinze ans.

16 : seize ans

In Great Britain: En Grande-Bretagne

= In France, we have to take an exam at 15.

Mes affaires — My stuff

Learn this short list of stuff you find in your school bag — and I'm not talking about half-eaten sandwiches, an unwashed P.E. kit, or the crumpled-up newsletter you should have given your mum last week.

pencil:	un crayon	*exercise book:*	un cahier
pen:	un stylo	*(text) book:*	un livre
calculator:	une calculatrice	*school bag:*	un cartable
ruler:	une règle		

School rules — not as far as I'm concerned...

Details, details and more details — they're vital for this section. Close the book and see how many you can remember — the more you can reel off about your school, the better. It's weird, but French people will love to hear about your uniform, since they don't have them — pretty unfair.

Classroom Language

We all have our 'off' days, so it's really useful to be able to ask someone to repeat something, or spell out a word you're not sure about. It could get you out of a sticky hole in your speaking assessment.

Asseyez-vous! — Sit down!

Learn these 4 phrases to avoid teacherly wrath. The 'vous' ones are formal and the 'tu' ones are informal.

Levez-vous! = Stand up!

Lève-toi! = Stand up!

Asseyez-vous! = Sit down!

Assieds-toi! = Sit down!

For more on the difference between 'tu' and 'vous' see page 5

Parlez-vous français? — Do you speak French?

We all make mistakes and misunderstand things sometimes, but if you can ask for help you just might never make the same mistake twice. So this stuff can help you understand better — it's really worth learning.

Comment ça s'écrit? = How do you spell that?

Comment est-ce qu'on dit ça en français? = How do you say that in French?

Pouvez-vous répéter, s'il vous plaît? = Can you repeat that, please?

If you don't understand, say 'Je ne comprends pas'

These phrases can be vital in your speaking assessments. Even if the worst happens, it's far better to say 'I don't understand' in French than to shrug, give a cheesy smile and mumble something in English.

Je (ne) comprends (pas). = I (don't) understand.

Qu'est-ce que ça veut dire? = What does that mean?

Pouvez-vous expliquer ce mot? = Can you explain this word? (formal)

Can you (informal): Peux-tu

Est-ce que j'ai fait une erreur? — Did I make a mistake?

Je ne sais pas. = I don't know.

Je me suis trompé(e). = I was wrong.

C'est vrai. = That's right.

C'est faux. = That's wrong.

Tu as raison. = You're right.

Tu as tort. = You're wrong.

"Comment ça s'écrit?" — "Ç-A"

You can save yourself from an embarrassing silence by asking the person you're talking to if they can repeat or clarify something — there's no shame in it. All you have to do is learn these dead useful phrases. Remember, bouts of forgetfulness happen to everyone — DON'T PANIC.

Problems at School

If you're anything like me, you love to complain about stuff — this is your chance. This page gives you all sorts of ways to vent your school-related stresses and gripes. So go on — indulge...

L'école, c'est difficile — School's difficult

Est-ce que tout va bien au lycée? = Is everything going well at school?

Oui, tout va bien. = Yes, everything's going well.

Non, j'ai beaucoup de problèmes à l'école. = No, I've got lots of problems at school.

J'ai de bonnes notes mais je n'ai pas le temps de sortir le soir. = I get good marks, but I don't have time to go out in the evening.

Au collège je ne finis jamais mon travail.

I have difficulties understanding: j'ai des difficultés à comprendre

= At school I never finish my work.

On doit porter un uniforme démodé et on n'a pas le droit de porter du maquillage.

= We have to wear an old-fashioned uniform and we aren't allowed to wear make-up.

Je suis inquiet / inquiète — I'm worried

Je travaille beaucoup mais ce n'est pas assez pour mes parents.

= I work a lot, but it's not enough for my parents.

Mes parents pensent que je dois étudier tout le temps.

= My parents think I should study all the time.

Les profs ne m'aiment pas. = The teachers don't like me.

I have to study all the time for the exams.

Assez 'stressed', you say 'out' — Stressed, out, stressed, out

Frankly, it would be dull if everyone said everything was great all the time. This stuff's tricky, but really worth learning. Then you can get it all off your chest, just like a proper therapy session.

Work Experience

These pages make you think even more about your future — it's nearly a public service. If you can't see your future without the aid of a crystal ball, then start exercising your imagination.

As-tu fait un stage? — Have you done work experience?

Work experience is great — I remember my week spent bored to death in a certain high street bank...

J'ai fait mon stage en entreprise chez Peugeot. = I did my work experience at Peugeot.

Put any company name here.

J'ai travaillé chez Peugeot pendant une semaine. = I worked at Peugeot for a week.

Je n'ai jamais fait un stage. = I have never done work experience.

haven't yet: n'ai pas encore

Est-ce que tu as aimé le travail? — Did you like the work?

More opinions wanted — own up, did you or did you not like it?

Le travail était amusant. = The work was fun.

boring: ennuyeux
interesting: intéressant

Mes collègues de travail n'étaient pas sympa. = My colleagues were unfriendly.

were friendly: étaient sympathiques
were interesting: étaient intéressants

Ce n'était pas facile — It wasn't easy...

Imagine now that your work experience job is your career for life. Does that change your opinions?

Les horaires sont terribles. = The hours are terrible.

great: géniaux fantastic: fantastiques

Ce n'est pas très bien payé. = It's not very well paid.

It is: C'est

J'ai un boulot — I have a job

Make this easier by choosing easy-to-say jobs and simple values — if only the rest of life was like that.

Je travaille tous les samedis dans un supermarché. = I work every Saturday in a supermarket.

weekends: les week-ends

Je gagne cinq livres par heure. = I earn £5 per hour.

£15 per week: quinze livres par semaine

You can find plenty more jobs on page 72.

Are you experienced?...

You might have to comment on your work experience or part-time jobs in the speaking assessment. Talk about anything work-related that you've done in your life, and give your opinions about it too.

Plans for the Future

If your idea of future plans is what you're doing next weekend, then try thinking a bit further ahead...

L'année prochaine... — Next year...

There are loads of things to do after GCSEs. Here's the basic vocab.

Je voudrais préparer le bac. = I would like to do A-levels.

'Bac' is short for 'Baccalauréat', the French equivalent of A-levels — except that they do more subjects than we do.

to study geography: étudier la géographie.

J'ai choisi d'entrer en première au lycée parce que ... = I've chosen to go into the Sixth Form at school because...

I have some good friends there: j'ai de bon(ne)s ami(e)s là.
I can do my favourite subjects: je peux faire mes matières préférées.

J'ai décidé de quitter l'école. = I've decided to leave school.

Je voudrais faire un stage en entreprise. = I'd like to do work experience at a company.

get married and have children: me marier et avoir des enfants.

Je vais chercher un emploi. = I'm going to look for a job.

If you would like to do a particular job after school, use the phrases from page 73.

Je vais voyager. = I'm going to travel.

Give short, sharp reasons for your answers

When you're commenting on your future plans, keeping explanations short, clear and simple helps stop you from making silly mistakes. Try some of the following:

For more school subjects see page 65.

Je voudrais étudier la musique, parce que je veux devenir musicien(ne). = I would like to study music, because I want to be a musician.

maths: les maths (fem.) *I.T.:* l'informatique (fem.)

engineer: ingénieur *teacher:* prof(esseur)

Je voudrais préparer le bac car je veux étudier la biologie à l'université. = I would like to do A-levels because I want to study biology at university.

"I'll be bac..."

I know GCSE French seems like a scary mystery, but this sort of stuff comes up year after year... Learn all this and you'll be laughing. Use words like 'je voudrais' and 'parce que' for extra marks.

Types of Job

There are more jobs here than you can shake a stick at — and you do need to recognise all of them because any of the little blighters could pop up in your listening and reading exams.

Female versions of jobs can be tricky

Often, job titles in French are different for men and women. You need to recognise both versions...

Masculine/Feminine

Watch out for the feminine versions of jobs. Although there are lots which just add an 'e' in the feminine, some follow different rules. For example, '-er' often becomes 'ère,' '-teur' often becomes '-trice' and '-eur' often becomes '-euse.' If you're not sure, check in a dictionary.

Le boucher (masc.)	La bouchère (fem.)	= Butcher
L'acteur (masc.)	L'actrice (fem.)	= Actor / actress
Le coiffeur (masc.)	La coiffeuse (fem.)	= Hairdresser

The gender of a job depends on who is doing it

You'll need to recognise all these, too:

X-facteur

GET-YOUR-HANDS-DIRTY JOBS

mechanic:	le mécanicien, la mécanicienne
electrician:	l'électricien, l'électricienne
plumber:	le/la plombier
chef:	le cuisinier, la cuisinière
baker:	le boulanger, la boulangère
farmer:	le fermier, la fermière
engineer:	l'ingénieur

MEDICAL JOBS

nurse:	l'infirmier, l'infirmière
doctor:	le médecin
dentist:	le/la dentiste

The gender of the job is always masculine (le) for a man and feminine (la) for a woman — except for 'le médecin', 'le professeur' and 'l'ingénieur', which are masculine for both.

A LOAD MORE JOBS

salesperson:	le vendeur, la vendeuse
waiter/waitress:	le serveur, la serveuse
head teacher:	le directeur, la directrice
policeman/woman:	le policier, la policière
postman/woman:	le facteur, la factrice
primary teacher:	l'instituteur, l'institutrice
secondary school teacher:	le professeur
air hostess:	l'hôtesse de l'air (fem.)
air steward:	le steward de l'air
cashier:	le caissier, la caissière
secretary:	le/la secrétaire
musician:	le musicien, la musicienne

OTHER JOB SITUATIONS

student:	l'étudiant(e)
apprentice:	l'apprenti(e)
housewife/househusband:	la femme de ménage, l'homme au foyer

Good job you've learnt all this...

Not nice. But start with the jobs you find easiest — then learn the rest. Try writing them down, reading them out loud, making up silly word games... try anything that'll get them learnt. Female versions too — ooh, I don't envy you. But think how knowledgeable you'll be at the end of it all.

Jobs: Advantages and Disadvantages

What a page title... It pretty much sums up what's important here, I think.

Say what job you'd like to do and why

Use 'devenir' (to become) to say what job you'd like to do.

State the job you'd like to do with a short and simple reason why — easy.

I hope: J'espère

Je voudrais devenir médecin...

= I would like to become a doctor...

For more words to say what you think of something, see pages 7-8.

... parce que le travail serait intéressant.

See page 72 for more jobs.

varied: varié *fun:* amusant *easy:* facile

= ... because the work would be interesting.

Je n'aimerais pas être... — I wouldn't like to be...

Je n'aimerais pas être plombier.

= I wouldn't like to be a plumber.

You can put any job from page 72 here.

Le travail est trop difficile.

= The work is too difficult.

tiring: fatigant *badly paid:* mal payé

Tu voudrais travailler à l'étranger? — Would you like to work abroad?

The world's your oyster...

Oui, j'aimerais trouver un boulot en France.

See page 41 for a list of countries. Remember 'au' for masculine countries.

= I would like to find a job in France.

Non, je n'aimerais pas travailler à l'étranger. J'ai peur de me sentir seul(e).

= No, I wouldn't like to work abroad. I'm afraid of feeling lonely.

Après le bac, je veux aller en France pour ....

= After A-levels, I want to go to France to...

study at university: étudier à l'université:
work in a restaurant: travailler dans un restaurant

I'll take the pros and leave the cons...

Valuable stuff. Saying what job you want to do and why is pretty essential. If the truth's too hard to say, if you want, say, a job in inverse-polarity-dynamo maintenance, then use something simpler. Don't forget these little bits and pieces for the assessments — they could be useful...

Getting a Job

Ah, getting a job... what it's all about. Slog now. Slog later. Bet you really feel like learning now...

Je cherche un emploi... — I'm looking for a job...

Je cherche un emploi dans un hôtel. = I'm looking for a job in a hotel.

a restaurant: un restaurant — *an office:* un bureau
a leisure centre: un centre de loisirs — *a shop:* un magasin

J'ai déjà travaillé dans un hôtel. = I've already worked in a hotel.

Je serais parfait(e) pour ce poste parce que je suis pratique. = I'd be perfect for this job because I'm practical.

I speak English / French / Italian / Spanish: je parle anglais / français / italien / espagnol.
I like working with children / people: j'aime travailler avec les enfants / les gens.

I am hard-working: je suis travailleur / travailleuse.
I am always bubbly: je suis toujours plein(e) de vie.

On cherche... — We are looking for...

See page 19 for more character traits.

On cherche un serveur / une serveuse
Lundi et vendredi soir
19 - 21:00

= We're looking for a waiter/waitress. Monday and Friday evening. 7 - 9pm.

Vous aimez travailler avec les enfants?
On cherche un(e) assistant(e).
20 heures par semaine.
Appelez Jean au
033 12-24-38-42

= Do you like working with children? We're looking for an assistant. 20 hours per week. Call Jean on 033 12-24-38-42

On cherche quelqu'un pratique, travailleur(euse), et aimable pour vendre et organiser.
Entrez pour plus de détails.

= We're looking for someone practical, hard-working and nice to sell products and organise. Come in for more details.

Je m'intéresse au poste... — I'm interested in the job...

So, you've applied. Hopefully they'll call back and say something like this:

Est-ce que vous pouvez venir nous voir ... = Can you come and see us...

and meet us: nous rencontrer
and meet the boss: rencontrer le patron

... lundi le 14 février à 10h? = ...on Monday, 14th February at 10am?

Apportez votre CV, s'il vous plaît. = Please bring your CV.

your passport: votre passeport (masc.)
your driving licence: votre permis de conduire (masc.)

Interested in the post? Cat called Jess...?

We've got just the job for you. Useful stuff this — rip this page out, pop it in a rucksack and go and get a summer job in Paris. No ripping 'til it's learnt, though — you've got exams to pass first...

Getting a Job

Good covering letter, dazzling CV, nice tie, job's yours.

J'ai lu votre annonce — I read your advertisement

Every job application needs a good letter...

Rachael Johnson
46 Loxley Road,
Ambridge,
Borsetshire. BO12 2AM

Madame de Villiers
Commerce Tapisserie,
19 rue du Conquérant,
14066 Bayeux

See p.11 for more on writing formal letters.

Madame, Bayeux, le 8 février 2009

J'ai lu votre annonce dans *Le Monde* hier, et je m'intéresse au poste de secrétaire.

Depuis deux ans je travaille comme secrétaire pour une petite entreprise à Londres. J'aime bien ce poste mais maintenant je voudrais travailler pour une entreprise plus grande.

Si vous avez besoin de plus de détails, n'hésitez pas de me demander.

Je vous prie d'agréer, Madame, l'expression de mes sentiments distingués.

Rachael Johnson

I read your advertisement in *Le Monde* yesterday, and I'm interested in the position of secretary.

For two years I've worked as a secretary for a small company in London. I like the job but now I'd like to work for a bigger company.

If you need more details, don't hesitate to ask me.

Voudriez-vous voir mon CV? — Would you like to see my CV?

And every applicant needs a good CV...

CURRICULUM VITAE

Rachael Johnson
46 Loxley Road, Ambridge, Borsetshire. BO12 2AM
Téléphone 02 40 54 10 66
Nationalité anglaise

ÉDUCATION
2005: A' levels (équivalence Baccalauréat):
Histoire (B), Anglais (B), Mathématiques (C)

EXPÉRIENCE PROFESSIONNELLE
Depuis 2007: Secrétaire chez 'Sales Albion', Loxley.
2005-2007: Caissière

AUTRES RENSEIGNEMENTS
Permis de conduire
Je parle anglais, français et gallois.

EDUCATION
2005: A levels (equivalent to Bac)
History (B), English (B), Maths (C)

PROFESSIONAL EXPERIENCE
Since 2007: Secretary at 'Sales Albion', Loxley.
2005-2007: Cashier

OTHER INFORMATION
Driving licence
I speak English, French and Welsh.

Et une belle cravate...

Work — a necessary part of life, alas, and a necessary part of GCSE French. Work / job-related tasks could crop up anywhere, so it's a good idea to get all this stuff well and truly off pat.

Telephones

You have to know French phone vocab and understand messages and stuff — it's simple. No. Really it is.

Au télephone — On the phone

This is easy marks — learn it...

Use 'ton' for someone you know well. If you need to be more formal, use 'votre'.

Quel est ton numéro de téléphone? = What is your telephone number?

Mon numéro de téléphone est le vingt-huit, dix-neuf, cinquante-six. = My telephone number is 28 19 56.

Put your phone number here — as 2-digit numbers, e.g. twenty-eight rather than two-eight.

See page 1 for all the numbers.

When you make a call, say 'ici Bob' — 'It's Bob here'

You need to be able to understand the general phone vocab used in France...

You might hear this when someone answers the phone: *Allô! C'est Philippe à l'appareil.* = Hello! Philippe speaking.

These questions are common phone enquiries: *Est-ce que Bob est là?* = Is Bob there?

Est-ce que je peux parler à Joanie ? = Can I speak to Joanie?

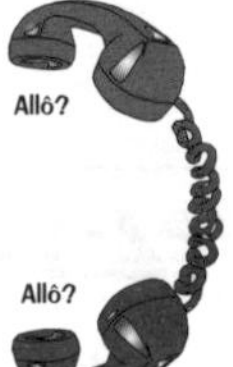

These are common conversation closers:

À bientôt. = See you soon.

Appelle-moi. = Call me.

Je voudrais laisser un message — I'd like to leave a message

You have to be able to understand phone messages. This is a typical run-of-the-mill one:

Allô, ici Nicole Smith. = Hello, this is Nicole Smith.

J'ai un message pour Jean-Claude. = I have a message for Jean-Claude.

Est-ce qu'il peut me rappeler vers dix-neuf heures ce soir? = Can he call me back at around 7pm this evening?

See page 2 for times.

Mon numéro de téléphone est le cinquante-neuf, dix-huit, quarante-sept. = My phone number is 59 18 47.

See page 1 for numbers.

Merci beaucoup. Au revoir. = Thank you very much. Goodbye.

Le téléphone — sounds phoney to me...

I wouldn't rate your chances with French GCSE if you don't learn this stuff — phones come up pretty frequently. But, with this lot under your belt, you'll have more than a fighting chance.

Revision Summary

This page is not important in the slightest. You don't have to stop and spend a second here. Keep on trekking matey... Except that this is an extremely important page. You do have to stop and spend some seconds here and you should only trek on when you know all of this stuff effortlessly. Capisce... That's foreign for 'Do you understand?' (And I know, I'd make a rubbish Soprano.)

1) Say what all your GCSE subjects are in French. I guess one of them will be 'le français'...
2) What is your favourite subject? What subject(s) don't you like? Answer in French.
3) Depuis quand apprends-tu le français? Translate the question. And then answer it in French.
4) How would you say that your lunch break begins at 12.30pm and that during lunch you talk to your friends?
5) How would you say that you have six lessons every day and each lesson lasts 50 minutes?
6) Pete is describing his school to his French penfriend Christophe. How would he say that there are three terms, that he wears a school uniform and that there are lots of rules?
7) Au collège, on n'a pas le droit de porter les baskets et on ne peut pas parler dans les couloirs. Your French friend has just told you this in her latest email. What does she say?
8) Describe your school uniform.
9) Your teacher has just said a very long sentence in French and you don't understand. What two questions could you ask to help clarify the situation?
10) Stéphanie says 'J'ai des difficultés à comprendre au collège. Les profs ne m'aiment pas parce que je ne finis jamais mon travail.' What does she mean?
11) Write a full French sentence explaining where you did your work experience. If you didn't do work experience anywhere then write that down.
12) What are your plans for after your GCSEs? Tell someone (in French).
13) Tell a French passer-by what job you'd most like to do and why.
14) Complete this tiebreaker question (in no more than 30 French words): Je suis parfait(e) pour ce poste parce que...
15) Translate into French: "I'm looking for a job in a restaurant. I have worked in a café for a year."
16) What's your phone number? *(No cheating and writing it in numerals — do it in French. And say it out loud.)*
17) What would you say in French when:
    a) you answer the phone in French?
    b) you want to tell someone you'll see them soon?
    c) you want to tell someone to call you?
    d) you have a message for Daniel Craig?

NOUNS

Words for People and Objects

Stop — before you panic, this stuff is a lot less scary than it looks. It's all pretty simple stuff about words for people and objects — nouns. This is really important.

Every French noun is masculine or feminine

Whether a word is masculine, feminine, singular or plural affects a heck of a lot of things. All 'the' and 'a' words change and, if that wasn't enough, the adjectives (like 'new', 'shiny') change to fit the word.

EXAMPLES: an interesting book: un livre intéressant (masculine)
an interesting programme: une émission intéressante (feminine)

For details on changing stuff like this, see pages 80 and 81.

It's no good just knowing the French words for things — you have to know whether each one's masculine or feminine too...

THE GOLDEN RULE

Each time you learn a word, remember a le or la to go with it — don't think 'dog = chien', think 'dog = le chien'.

LE AND LA

LE in front of a noun means it's masculine. LA in front = feminine.

These rules help you guess what gender a word is

If you have to guess whether a word is masculine or feminine, these are good rules of thumb.

RULES OF THUMB FOR MASCULINE AND FEMININE NOUNS

MASCULINE NOUNS (LE):
most nouns that end:
-age -er -eau -ing -ment -ou
-ail -ier -et -isme -oir -eil
also: male people, languages, days, months, seasons

FEMININE NOUNS (LA):
most nouns that end:
-aine -ée -ense -ie -ise -tion
-ance -elle -esse -ière -sion -tude
-anse -ence -ette -ine -té -ure
also: female people

Making Nouns Plural

1) Nouns in French are usually made plural by adding an 's' — just like English, really.

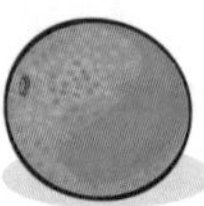

e.g.: une orange → des oranges
an orange → oranges

2) But there are always exceptions to the rule in French. Nouns with the endings in the table below have a different plural form — and this lot are just the beginning.

Noun ending	Irregular plural ending	Example
-ail	-aux	travail → travaux
-al	-aux	journal → journaux
-eau	-eaux	bureau → bureaux
-eu	-eux	jeu → jeux
-ou	-oux	chou → choux

TOP TIP FOR PLURALS

Each time you learn a word, make sure you know how to make it plural.

3) Some nouns have completely irregular plurals, e.g.: œil → yeux (eye → eyes). You'll have to learn these nouns by practising them over and over.
4) Some nouns don't change in the plural. These are usually nouns that end in -s, -x or -z.
5) When you make a noun plural, instead of 'le' or 'la' to say 'the', you have to use 'les' — see page 79.

un nez → des nez
a nose → noses
un fils → des fils
a son → sons

Masculine words — butch, hunky, stud...

The bottom line is — every time you learn a word in French, you have to learn whether it's le or la, and you have to learn how to make it plural. So start as you mean to go on — get into genders.

'The' and 'A'

ARTICLES

'The' and 'a' — you use these words more than a mobile phone. They're tricky. Revise 'em well.

'A' — un, une

1) In English we don't have genders for nouns — simple.
2) In French, you need to know whether a word is masculine or feminine.

masculine	feminine
un	une

EXAMPLES:

Masculine *J'ai un frère.* = I have a brother.

Feminine *J'ai une sœur.* = I have a sister.

'The' — le, la, l', les

1) Like the French for 'a', the word for 'the' is different for masculine and feminine. This one has a plural form as well, though.
2) For words starting with a vowel (a, e, i, o, u) the 'le' or 'la' are shortened to l', e.g. l'orange.
3) Some words starting with an 'h', also take 'l'' instead of 'le' or 'la'. Sadly there's no rule for this — you just have to learn which ones take 'l'' and which ones take 'le' or 'la'.

masculine singular	feminine singular	in front of a vowel /some words beginning with 'h'	masculine or feminine plural
le	la	l'	les

EXAMPLES:

Le garçon. = The boy.

La fille. = The girl.

L'homme. = The man.

Les hommes. = The men.

Le hamster. = The hamster.

Les hamsters. = The hamsters

'De' and 'à' change before 'le' and 'les'

1) Weird stuff happens with 'à' (to) and 'de' (of).
2) You can't say 'à le', 'à les', 'de le' or 'de les'.
3) 'À' and 'de' combine with 'le' and 'les' to make new words — 'au', 'aux' (meaning 'to the'), and 'du' and 'des' (meaning 'of the').

	le	la	l'	les
à +	au	à la	à l'	aux
de +	du	de la	de l'	des

EXAMPLES : *Je vais à* + *le café* = *Je vais au café.* = I go to the café.

Je viens de + *le Canada* = *Je viens du Canada.* = I come from Canada.

'Some' or 'any' — du, de la, de l', des

These don't just mean 'of the' — they can also mean 'some' or 'any'.

EXAMPLES:

J'ai des pommes. = I have some apples.

Avez-vous du pain? = Have you got any bread?

masculine singular	feminine singular	in front of a vowel / 'h' which takes 'l''	masculine or feminine plural
du	de la	de l'	des

N.B. In negative sentences, like 'I don't have any apples', you just use 'de' — 'Je n'ai pas de pommes'.

Any joy — thought not...

Phew, am I glad I speak English — just one word for 'the' and no genders (in grammar anyway). But there's no getting around it — you need this stuff to get your French right in the assessments. Cover up the page and write out all four tables — keep on scribbling till you can do it in your sleep.

ADJECTIVES

Words to Describe Things

Gain more marks and show what an interesting person you are by using some juicy describing words.

Adjectives must 'agree' with the thing they're describing

1) In English, the describing word (adjective) stays the same — like big bus, big bananas...
2) In French, the describing word has to change to match whether what it's describing is masculine or feminine and singular or plural. Look at these examples where 'intéressant' has to change:

Masculine Singular	Masculine Plural	Feminine Singular	Feminine Plural
le garçon intéressant	les garçons intéressants	la fille intéressante	les filles intéressantes
(the interesting boy)	(the interesting boys)	(the interesting girl)	(the interesting girls)

The Rules Are:

"You stink!" "I agree"

1. Add an '-e' to the describing word if the word being described is feminine (see page 78). ← Only if the describing word doesn't already end in 'e'.

2. Add an '-s' to the describing word if the word being described is plural (see page 78).

(Of course, that means if it's feminine plural, then you have to add '-es'.)

IMPORTANT NOTE: When you look an adjective up in the dictionary it gives the masculine singular form. Don't ask me why — it must have been a load of single blokes who wrote the dictionary.

Learn the describing words which don't follow the rules

1) Adjectives which end in -x, -f, -er, -on, -en, -el, -il and -c follow different rules:

Adjectives ending in these letters double their last letter before adding 'e' in the feminine.

Group of words ending:	Most important ones in the group	masculine singular	feminine singular	masculine plural	feminine plural
-x	ennuyeux (boring), délicieux (delicious), dangereux (dangerous), merveilleux (marvellous) & heureux →	heureux (happy)	heureuse	heureux	heureuses
-f	neuf (brand new) & sportif →	sportif (sporty)	sportive	sportifs	sportives
-er	dernier (last), cher (dear) & premier →	premier (first)	première	premiers	premières
-on, -en, -el, -il	mignon (sweet), ancien (old/former) gentil (kind) & bon →	bon (good)	bonne	bons	bonnes
-c	sec (dry) & blanc →	blanc (white)	blanche	blancs	blanches

'Sèche' (f.sing.) and 'sèches' (f.pl.) add an accent.

2) There are also some adjectives which are completely irregular — you'll have to learn these ones off by heart.

masculine singular	before a m. sing. noun beginning with a vowel or 'h' which takes 'l'	feminine singular	masculine plural	feminine plural
vieux (old)	vieil	vieille	vieux	vieilles
beau (fine/pretty)	bel	belle	beaux	belles
nouveau (new)	nouvel	nouvelle	nouveaux	nouvelles
long (long)	long	longue	longs	longues
tout (all)	tout	toute	tous	toutes

Quelque and chaque — rule-breakers...

'Quelque' only changes from singular to plural, by adding an 's' There is no difference for masc. and fem.

I bought some sweets:
J'ai acheté quelques bonbons.

'Chaque' always stays the same.

Every person here likes chocolate:
Chaque personne ici aime le chocolat.

Even 'désagréable(s)' agrees...

Aaaargh — more tables to learn, but then that's the nature of French grammar. For these endings to be of any use to you, you need to learn the genders of the nouns in the first place — you have to know what your adjective needs to agree with. To get it right, get learning.

Words to Describe Things

ADJECTIVES

Details and descriptions are key to doing well in the exams — so words to describe things are important.

Top 21 Describing Words

Here are 21 describing words (adjectives) — they're the ones you really have to know.

good:	bon(ne)	*interesting:*	intéressant(e)	*young:*	jeune
bad:	mauvais(e)	*boring:*	ennuyeux / ennuyeuse	*new:*	nouveau / nouvelle
beautiful:	beau / belle	*terrible:*	affreux / affreuse	*brand new:*	neuf / neuve
happy:	heureux / heureuse	*long:*	long(ue)	*fast:*	rapide
sad:	triste	*small/short:*	petit(e)	*slow:*	lent(e)
easy:	facile	*big/tall:*	grand(e)	*practical:*	pratique
difficult:	difficile	*old:*	vieux / vieille	*strange:*	étrange

Most describing words go after the word they describe

It's the opposite of English — in French most describing words go after the word they're describing.

EXAMPLES:

J'ai une voiture rapide. = I have a fast car.

J'ai lu un livre intéressant. = I read an interesting book.

la robe rouge — noun (dress), adjective (red)

You can also use describing words in sentences with verbs like 'être' (to be) and 'devenir' (to become). The adjective still needs to agree with the noun though.

Adjectives are always masculine singular after 'ce'. E.g. 'C'est nouveau' (It's new), 'C'était cher' (It was expensive), etc.

EXAMPLES:

Ils sont heureux. = They are happy.

Les légumes sont bons, mais le chocolat est meilleur. = Vegetables are good, but chocolate is better.

'Meilleur' is the comparative form of 'bon' — it's another way of saying 'plus bon'. For more on comparatives, see page 84.

There are some odd ones out that go in front

These describing words almost always go before the noun — a real pain:

good:	bon(ne)	*young:*	jeune	*bad:*	mauvais(e)
fine / pretty:	beau / belle	*old:*	vieux / vieil(le)	*high:*	haut(e)
better / best:	meilleur(e)	*nice / pretty:*	joli(e)	*big/tall:*	grand(e)
new:	nouveau / nouvel(le)	*small:*	petit(e)	*first:*	premier/première

EXAMPLES: *J'ai un nouveau chat.* = I have a new cat.

J'ai une petite maison, avec un joli jardin et une belle vue.

= I have a small house, with a pretty garden and a beautiful view.

Adjectives still have to agree, regardless of whether they come before or after the noun.

Good, bad... indifferent?

By now you're probably thinking you could get through life without adjectives and you could well be right — as long as you never want to tell anyone how interesting, beautiful and happy you are. Start by learning those 21 key words at the top of the page — they'll spice your writing up no end.

ADJECTIVES

Words to Describe Things

More really important stuff on describing words, including words that show who something belongs to...

Some mean different things before and after the noun

Some adjectives change their meaning according to whether they are before or after the noun. Here are some important ones — learn them carefully:

adjective	meaning if before		meaning if after	
ancien	former	un ancien soldat (a former soldier)	old/ancient	un homme ancien (an old man)
cher	dear	mon cher ami (my dear friend)	expensive	une voiture chère (an expensive car)
propre	own	ma propre chambre (my own room)	clean	ma chambre propre (my clean room)

My, your, our — words for who it belongs to

You have to be able to use and understand these words to say that something belongs to someone:

Like in English, these go before the noun. E.g. 'mon ami', 'notre cousin', etc.

You have to choose the gender (masculine, feminine or plural) to match the thing it's describing, and NOT the person it belongs to. So in the example below, it's always 'mon père' even if it's a girl talking.

	masculine singular	feminine singular	plural
my	mon	ma	mes
your (informal, sing.)	ton	ta	tes
his/her/its	son	sa	ses
our	notre	notre	nos
your (formal/pl.)	votre	votre	vos
their	leur	leur	leurs

Mon père est petit, ma mère est grande. = My father is short, my mother is tall.

This means that son/sa/ses could mean either 'his' or 'her'. You can usually tell which one it is just by using common sense.

J'ai vu Pierre avec sa sœur. = I saw Pierre with his sister.

Marie et sa sœur sont ennuyeuses. = Marie and her sister are boring.

'Ma amie' becomes 'mon amie'

Before a noun beginning with a vowel or words beginning with 'h', always use the masculine form. You do this because it's easier to say.

Mon amie s'appelle Helen. = My friend's called Helen.

Écoutez son histoire. Listen to his/her story.

My, oh my...

...what fun we're having. It's so important, all this — especially that the possessive adjectives change according to the thing being described, NOT the owner. And when you see words like 'cher', it should set a little bell ringing in your mind that it could have one of two meanings.

Words to Describe Actions

ADVERBS

The three previous pages describe objects, e.g. the bus is red. This page is about describing things you do, e.g. 'I speak French perfectly', and about adding more info — 'I speak French almost perfectly'.

Make your sentences better by saying how you do things

1) In English, you don't say 'I talk slow' — you have to add a 'ly' on the end to say 'I talk slowly'.
2) In French, you have to add a 'ment' on the end, but first you have to make sure the describing word is in the feminine form (see page 80).

EXAMPLES: *Il parle lentement.* = He speaks slowly.

normally: normalement

The French word for 'slow' is 'lent', but the feminine form is 'lente'. Add 'ment' and you get 'lentement' = slowly.

3) Unlike adjectives (pages 80-82) you don't ever have to change these words — they're describing the action, not the person doing it:

Always the same.

Feminine *Elle parle lentement.* Plural *Nous parlons lentement.*

Learn these odd ones out off by heart

Just like in English there are odd ones out — for example, you don't say 'I sing goodly'. The adjective 'good' changes to 'well' when it becomes an adverb. Have a look at the other odd ones out in the table:

ENGLISH	FRENCH
good → well	bon(ne) → bien
fast → fast	rapide → vite

Use one of these fine words to give even more detail

Add any one of these simple words or phrases to make that impressive sentence even more so... You can use them for sentences saying how something is done:

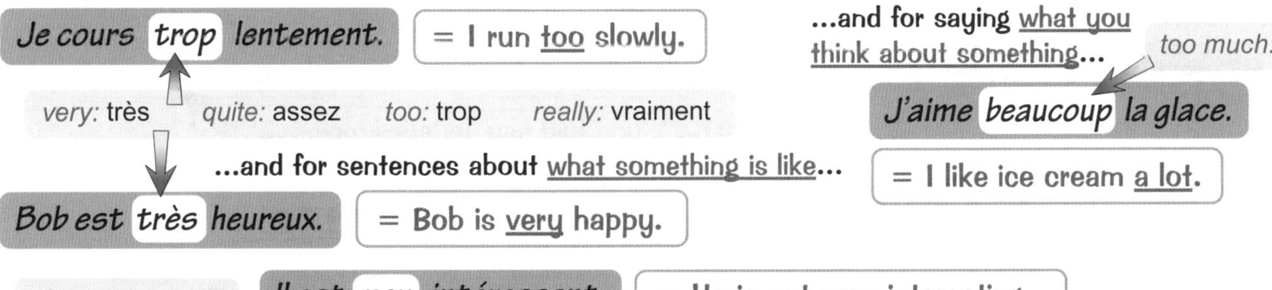

sometimes: quelquefois *often:* souvent

...and for saying how often something is done...

Je joue de temps en temps au football. = I play football from time to time.

Lentement — not how you act at Lent (that's fast)...

Alrighty — this is a bit like English — you have a set ending (-ment) to learn and stick on, and it's not too tricky either. Make sure you really know the standard rule and the couple of exceptions. Practise taking a few French sentences and adding detail... then use them in your assessments.

COMPARATIVES & SUPERLATIVES

Comparing Things

Often you don't just want to say that something is tasty, juicy or whatever — you want to say that it's the tastiest, or (to create a nice amount of jealousy) that it's juicier than someone else's...

How to say more weird, most weird

In French you can't say 'stranger' or 'strangest' — you have to say 'more strange' or 'most strange':

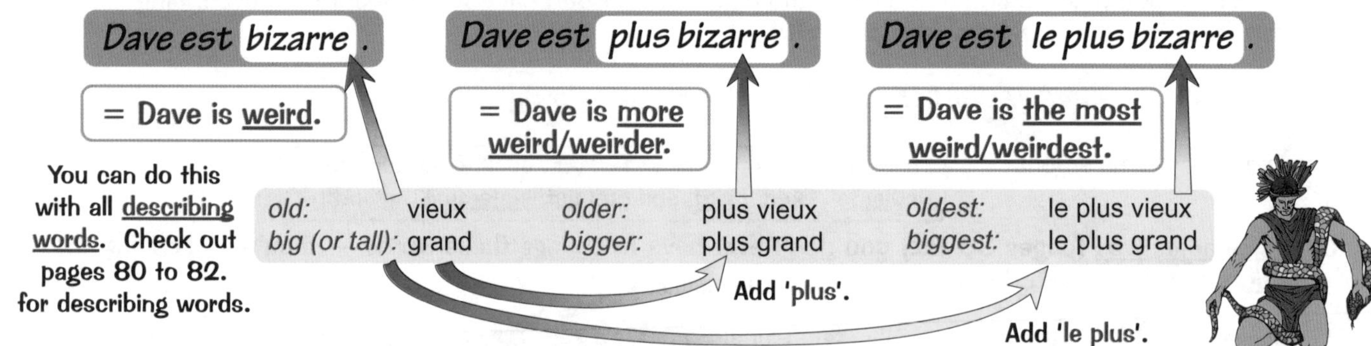

Dave est bizarre.
= Dave is weird.
Dave est plus bizarre.
= Dave is more weird/weirder.
Dave est le plus bizarre.
= Dave is the most weird/weirdest.
old: vieux
big (or tall): grand
older: plus vieux
bigger: plus grand
oldest: le plus vieux
biggest: le plus grand
Add 'plus'.
Add 'le plus'.

You can do this with all describing words. Check out pages 80 to 82. for describing words.

Don't forget agreement

The adjectives still need to agree as normal:

less pretty: moins jolie
Cette robe est plus jolie.
= This dress is prettier.
less strong: moins forts
Ils sont plus forts.
= They're stronger.

'The most ...' is 'le plus', 'la plus' or 'les plus' — it must match the word you're describing (see page 79).

the least funny: la moins amusante
Liz est la plus forte.
= Liz is the strongest.
the least strong: les moins forts
Ils sont les plus forts.
= They are the strongest.

The two ways of comparing things — More and Less

If you want to say 'less ...', you just use the word 'moins' instead of 'plus'. And the word for 'than' is 'que'.

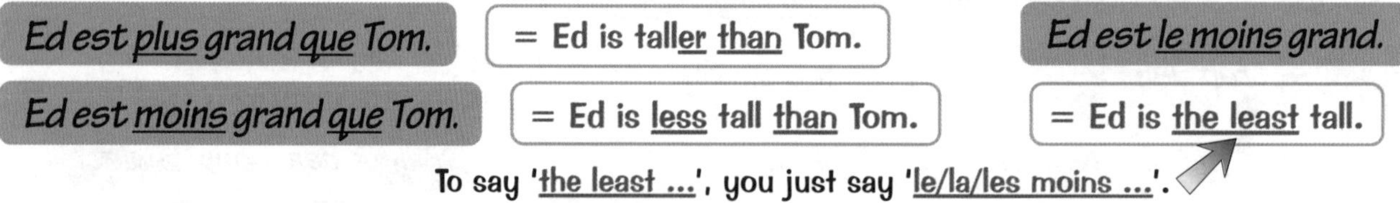

Ed est plus grand que Tom.
= Ed is taller than Tom.
Ed est moins grand que Tom.
= Ed is less tall than Tom.
Ed est le moins grand.
= Ed is the least tall.

To say 'the least ...', you just say 'le/la/les moins ...'.

More or most weirdly is pretty much the same...

When you're comparing how people do things, it works pretty much how you'd expect:

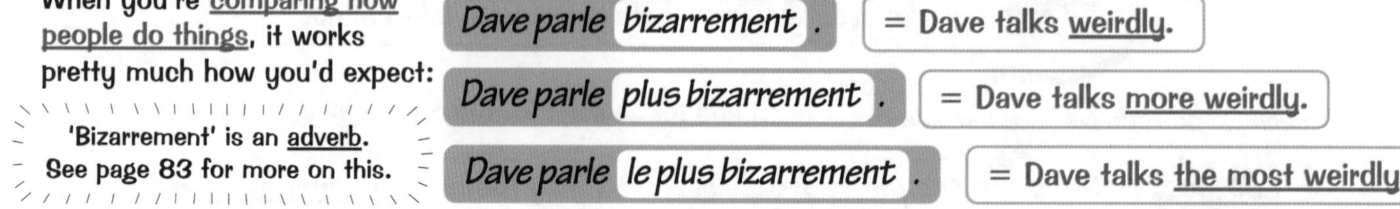

Dave parle bizarrement.
= Dave talks weirdly.
Dave parle plus bizarrement.
= Dave talks more weirdly.
Dave parle le plus bizarrement.
= Dave talks the most weirdly.

'Bizarrement' is an adverb. See page 83 for more on this.

Mirror, mirror on the wall...

Yup, the comparative is a favourite of wicked stepmothers and it's a favourite with French teachers too — they simply adore it when you get it right. To learn this kind of thing you just need to repeat some examples to yourself about 30 times in a kind of weird chant until it sticks.

Sneaky Wee Words

PREPOSITIONS

It all looks terrifying. But you've got to learn it if you want tip-top marks. It's only really a few words...

TO — à or en

Where we use 'to', the French usually use 'à': *Il va à Paris.* = He's going to Paris.

But for feminine countries and ones beginning with a vowel, it's usually 'en':

Il va en France. = He's going to France.

For things like to go, to do, just use the infinitive (see page 91) — you don't need an extra word for 'to'. E.g. aller = to go, faire = to make.

For 'the train to Calais' see 'the train for Calais' below. For times, like '10 to 4', see page 2.

ON — sur or à

For 'on top' of something, it's 'sur':

Sur la table. = On the table.

For days of the week, it's left out:

Je pars lundi. = I'm leaving on Monday.

When it's not 'on top', it's usually 'à':

Je l'ai vu à la télé. = I saw it on TV.

J'irai à pied. = I'll go on foot.

IN — dans, à or en

If it's actually inside something, then it's usually 'dans': *C'est dans la boîte.* = It's in the box.

If it's in a town, it's 'à': *J'habite à Marseille.* = I live in Marseilles.

If you want to say in a feminine country, or one beginning with a vowel, then it's usually 'en': *J'habite en France.* = I live in France.

FOR — pour or depuis

Where we use 'for', they usually use 'pour':

Un cadeau pour moi. = A present for me.

For 'the train for...', it's 'pour':

Le train pour Calais. = The train for Calais.

To say how long you're going to do something for in the future, use 'pour':

Je vais aller en France pour le week-end. = I'm going to go to France for the weekend.

To say things like 'I've studied French for 5 years', use the present tense (see page 92-93) and 'depuis':

J'apprends le français depuis cinq ans. = I've studied French for 5 years.

Tiny but deadly...

There's so much on this page that catches people out. Before carrying on, go back over this page and cover up all the boxes with French in them, and translate back all the English sentences.

PREPOSITIONS & INDEFINITE PRONOUNS

Sneaky Wee Words

A couple more sneaky words, and then a little bit on someone...

AT — à

À six heures. = At six o'clock.

Elle est à l'école. = She is at school.

Watch out: Sometimes it's hard to spot the 'à' in a sentence, because 'à + le = au' and 'à + les = aux' — see page 79.

FROM — de or à partir de

Where we use 'from', they usually use 'de':

De Londres à Paris. = From London to Paris.

Je viens de Cardiff. = I come from Cardiff.

For dates, it's 'à partir de':

À partir du 4 juin. = From the 4th of June.

Watch out: sometimes it's hard to spot the 'de' in a sentence, because 'de + le= du', and 'de + les = des' — see page 79.

OF — de or en

Where we use 'of', they usually use 'de': *Une bouteille de lait.* = A bottle of milk.

'Made of' is 'en': *C'est en coton.* = It's made of cotton.

Le 2 juin. = The 2nd of June.

You don't say 'of' with dates (see page 3):

French often also uses expressions ending in 'de' to talk about where something is:

À côté du parc. = Next to the park.

Au bout du jardin. = At the end of the garden.

Au-dessus du bar. = Above the bar.

Au fond de la rue. = At the end of the road.

Au dessous du café. = Below the cafe.

En face de la banque. = Opposite the bank.

SOMEONE — quelqu'un

J'ai vu quelqu'un que je connais. = I saw someone that I know.

Il y a quelqu'un? = Is someone there?

See, size does matter...

Who'd have thought it'd be the littlest words in the book that'd give you the most trouble? Still, we've reached the end of these diminutive horrors now — well, just as soon as you've learnt them.

I, You, Him, Them...

PRONOUNS

Pronouns are words that replace nouns — things like 'you', 'she' or 'them'.

je, tu, il, elle — I, you, he, she

You need 'I', 'you', 'he' and 'she' most often — to replace the subject (main person/thing) in a sentence...

Paul finally has a new job. He shaves poodles at the poodle parlour.

'He' is a pronoun. It means you don't have to say 'Paul' again.

THE SUBJECT PRONOUNS

I	je	nous	*we*
you (informal singular)	tu	vous	*you* (plural or formal)
he/it	il	ils	*they* (masc. or masc. & fem.)
she/it	elle	elles	*they* (all fem.)
one/we	on		

Le chien mange la brosse. = The dog eats the brush.

Il mange la brosse. = He eats the brush.

The French use 'on' frequently when talking about 'we'. E.g. 'On mange' = 'We eat', 'On va aller au cinéma' = 'We are going to go to the cinema.' It's a very useful pronoun.

Special words for me, you, him, her...

In some sentences, you need to emphasise exactly who is being talked about. For example, you can say 'he's taller', but you can make the sentence clearer using an emphatic pronoun, e.g. 'he's taller than you'. There are four occasions when you need to use emphatic pronouns in French:

EMPHATIC PRONOUNS

me	moi	*us*	nous
you (informal sing.)	toi	*you* (plural or formal)	vous
him/it	lui	*them* (masc. or masc. & fem.)	eux
her/it	elle	*them* (all fem.)	elles
one	soi		

1) Telling people to do something to you or to themselves.	*Écoutez-moi!* = Listen to me!
2) Comparing things.	*Il est plus grand que toi.* = He is taller than you.
3) After words like 'with', 'for', 'from'... (prepositions).	*Nous allons avec eux.* = We're going with them.
4) Where the words are on their own, or after 'c'est'.	*Qui parle? Moi! C'est moi!* = Who's speaking? Me! It's me!

For more on this, see page 101.

For more on comparing, see page 84.

For more on prepositions, see page 85-86.

When French people want to be even clearer about who's being talked about, e.g. 'I made this cake myself,' they use one of these words instead of a normal emphatic pronoun. They all mean '...-self' (myself, yourself, himself etc.).

moi-même, toi-même, lui-même, elle-même, soi-même, nous-mêmes, vous-mêmes, eux-mêmes, elles-mêmes

J'ai demandé à Sophie de promener le chien, mais j'ai rangé ma chambre moi-même.

= I asked Sophie to walk the dog, but I tidied my room myself.

Special words for me — you don't deserve them...

You're not going to get very far in the exams if you can't understand things like I, you, he, she and we. The good news is that it's pretty darn easy. You don't even have to learn any sentences on this page — just a few words you probably already know. You've got no excuse whatsoever. Hm.

PRONOUNS

Me, You, Him, Them, and En & Y

More pronouns. Yuck. The good news is, you only have to recognise the stuff on this page — you won't actually have to use any of it at all in your writing or speaking.

me, te, le, la — me, you, him, her

These are for the person/thing in a sentence that's having the action done to it (the direct object).

Dave lave le chien. = Dave washes the dog.

Dave (le) lave. = Dave washes it.

Dave lave la moto. = Dave washes the motorbike.

Dave (la) lave. = Dave washes it.

THE DIRECT OBJECT PRONOUNS

me	me	nous	*us*
you (inf. sing.)	te	vous	*you* (plural or formal)
him/it	le	les	*them*
her/it	la		

There are special words for to me, to her, to them

For things that need 'to' or 'for' — like writing to someone — use the indirect object pronouns.

THE INDIRECT OBJECT PRONOUNS

to me	me	nous	*to us*
to you (inf. sing.)	te	vous	*to you* (plural or formal)
to him/her/it	lui	leur	*to them*

Le chien donne la brosse à Dave. = The dog gives the brush to Dave.

Le chien (lui) donne la brosse. = The dog gives the brush to him.

Two Top Words — 'En' & 'Y'

EN — MEANING 'OF IT'

When 'en' comes before the verb, it usually translates as 'of it', 'of them', 'some' or 'any'. Verbs that need de after them, like 'avoir besoin de' replace the 'de' with 'en' to translate 'it' or 'them'. e.g. J'ai besoin de la banane. J'en ai besoin. I need the banana. → I need it.

Y — MEANING 'THERE'

E.g. J'y vais. I'm going there.
It's also used to mean 'it' or 'them' after verbs which are followed by à, e.g. penser à — to think about.
E.g. Je n'y pense pas. I don't think about it.

All Object Pronouns Go Before the Verb

These pronouns always go before the verb. If there are two object pronouns in the same sentence, they both go before the verb, but they go in a special order.

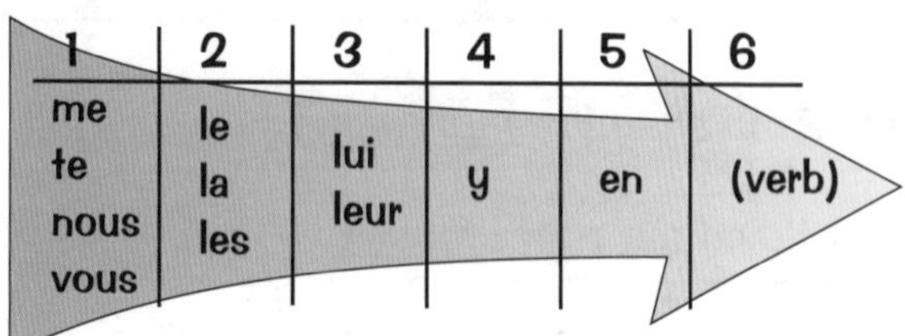

1
2
3
4
5
6
me te nous vous
le la les
lui leur
y
en
(verb)

Examples: Il me les donne. He gives them to me.
Je le lui ai donné. I gave it to him.

If there's a negative too, the 'ne' goes before the object pronoun(s), and the 'pas' after the verb.

Example: Je ne les mange pas. I don't eat them.

Useful expression using 'en' — j'en ai marre*...

This stuff is pretty grisly, I'll admit. You have to understand these when you see or hear them, but just because you don't need to use them doesn't mean you can just skip to the next page. Really understanding all this is the key to not being thrown by tricky sentences at exam time.

*I'm sick of it

This, That, Who and Which

Demonstratives & Relative Pronouns

Pointing things out in shops, and generally making it clear who you're on about, is important.

How to say this thing or these things

Use 'ce', 'cet'... in front of another word for saying things like 'this man', 'these apples' — i.e. when you're using 'this' as a describing word.

masculine singular	masculine singular before vowel or 'h' which takes 'l'	feminine singular	plural
ce	cet	cette	ces

EXAMPLES:

ce stylo: *this pen* — cet oiseau: *this bird*
cette maison: *this house* — ces pommes: *these apples*

Donne-moi ça — Give me that

If it's blatantly obvious what you're talking about, you don't need to refer to the object by name at all. Instead, you can say 'that' using 'ça,' or 'cela,' if you want to be really polite.

Je veux ça. = I want that. *Je veux cela.* = I want that.

Qui and que — Which / who / that...

These are probably the trickiest of the tricky French words. You only need to actually use 'qui' but if you see either of them in a sentence, you need to know who's doing what.

1) If you see 'qui', the person/thing at the start of the sentence is the person/thing that's doing the verb.

Un professeur qui aime bien sa classe.
= A teacher who likes his class.
person 'doing' the verb
verb
It's QUI, so it's the teacher that's doing the liking.

2) If you see 'que', then it's the person or thing that comes after the word 'que' that's doing the action described by the verb.

Un professeur que sa classe aime bien. = A teacher that his class likes.

person or thing 'doing' the verb — verb

It's QUE, so it's the class liking the teacher, NOT the teacher liking the class.

EXAMPLES:

Où est le bâtiment qu'il a vu? = Where is the building he saw? → QUE — so 'il' is doing the seeing.

Où est le chien qui courait? = Where is the dog that was running? → QUI — so the dog was doing the running.

So, what are you studying — oh, this and that...

Imagine you were in a French bakery and you wanted a big cream cake, but the shop assistant went to pick up the spinach puff next to it — you'd want to be able to jab your finger at the cream cake and say 'ÇA!', wouldn't you... In short, to avoid baked goods confusion, learn this.

CONJUNCTIONS

Joining Words — Longer Sentences

Everyone knows long sentences are clever — and clever people are popular when it's assessment-marking time. So learn these joining words to help you make longer sentences, and get more marks for being smart.

Et = And

J'aime jouer au football. AND *J'aime jouer au rugby.* = *J'aime jouer au football et au rugby.*

= I like playing football. / = I like playing rugby. / = I like playing football and rugby.

Ou = Or

This is different from 'où' (with an accent), which means 'where' — see page 4.

Il joue au football tous les jours. OR *Il joue au rugby tous les jours.* = *Il joue au football ou au rugby tous les jours.*

= He plays football every day. / = He plays rugby every day. / = He plays football or rugby every day.

Mais = But

J'aime jouer au football. BUT *Je n'aime pas jouer au rugby.* = *J'aime jouer au football mais je n'aime pas jouer au rugby.*

= I like playing football. / = I don't like playing rugby. / = I like playing football but I don't like playing rugby.

Parce que = Because

This is a really important one you need to use to explain yourself. There's loads more about it on page 8.

J'aime le tennis parce que c'est amusant. = I like tennis because it's fun.

Other wee joining words to understand

You don't have to use all of these, but you should understand them all...

EXAMPLES:

Tu peux sortir si tu veux. = You can go out if you want.

J'ai faim, donc je vais manger. = I'm hungry, so I'm going to eat.

Il est comme son frère. = He's like his brother.

Elle joue au hockey avec son amie. = She plays hockey with her friend.

See page 8 for more on 'car'.

because:	car
if:	si
with:	avec
as, like:	comme
so, therefore:	donc
while, during:	pendant (que)

But me no buts....

You use 'and', 'or' and 'but' all the time when you're speaking English — and if you don't use the equivalent words when you speak French, you'll sound a bit weird. But don't confuse 'ou' and 'où'. Try to recognise all the extra words in the last bit too, and, better still, use them.

The Lowdown on Verbs

Verbs, Tenses and the Infinitive

You have to know about verbs — you just can't get away from them.
Learn the stuff on this page to make the whole of GCSE French easier.

Verbs are action words — they tell you what's going on

These are verbs.

Ethel **plays** *football every Saturday.*

Alex **wished** *his grandma* **preferred** *knitting.*

And so is this.

There's a load of stuff you need to know about verbs, but it all boils down to these two things...

1) You have different words for different times

You say things differently if they happened last week, or aren't going to happen till tomorrow.

PAST	PRESENT	FUTURE
HAS ALREADY HAPPENED	HAPPENING NOW	HASN'T HAPPENED YET
I went to Tibet last year. I have been to Tibet. I had been to Tibet.	I am going to Tibet.	I go to Tibet on Monday. I will go to Tibet. I will be going to Tibet.

These are all different tenses, in case you're interested.

2) You have different words for different people

You say 'he plays', but you don't say 'I plays' — it'd be daft. You change the verb to fit the person.

ME DOING IT	YOU DOING IT	HIM DOING IT
I am eating parsnips or I eat parsnips.	You are eating parsnips or You eat parsnips.	He is eating parsnips or He eats parsnips.

OK, you get the picture — verbs are dead important. You use them all the time, so you need to learn all this stuff. That's why I've gone on about them so much on pages 92-104.

The word you look up in the dictionary means 'to...'

When you want to say 'I dance' in French, you start by looking up 'dance' in the dictionary. But you can't just use the first word you find — there's more to it than that...

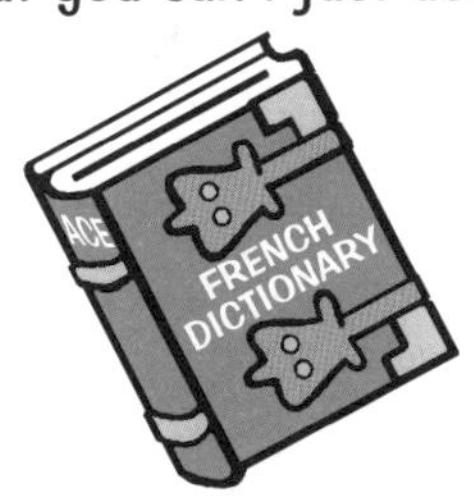

When you look up a verb in the dictionary, this is what you get:

For grammar fans, this is called the infinitive.

to give: donner
to go: aller

Most of the time you won't want to use the verb in its raw state — you'll have to change it so it's right for the person and time you're talking about.

There's loads about this on pages 92-104 — learn it all now, and you'll get it right in the assessments.

Ah, verbs — what would we do without them...

I'm not kidding — this is mega-important stuff. Over the next few pages I'll give you loads of stuff on verbs because there's loads you need to know. Some of it's easy, some of it's tricky — but if you don't understand the things on this page before you start, you'll have no chance.

PRESENT TENSE

Verbs in the Present Tense

The present tense mostly describes things that are happening now. You'll probably need it more than any other form of the verb, so it's really important.

The Present tense describes What's Happening Now

Present tense verbs describe either something that's happening now, e.g. 'I am brushing my teeth' or something which happens repeatedly, e.g. 'I brush my teeth every day'. There are 3 easy steps to put a verb into the present tense:

1) Get the infinitive of the verb you want, e.g. 'regarder'
2) Knock off the last two letters: regard~~er~~ This gives you the stem.
3) Add the new ending. This depends on the kind of verb and the person doing the verb (see below). E.g. Il regard**e**, vous regard**ez**, ils regard**ent**.

Examples of Present Tense Stems			
Infinitive	regarder	finir	vendre
Stem	regard	fin	vend

Endings for -er verbs

To form the present tense of regular '-er' verbs, add the endings shown to the verb's stem — e.g.:

The first bit ('regard') doesn't change. → *regarder = to watch*

See page 5 for when to use 'tu' and when to use 'vous'.

I watch = *je*	regard **e**	nous	regard **ons**	=	*we watch*
you (informal singular) watch = *tu*	regard **es**	vous	regard **ez**	=	*you (formal & plural) watch*
he/it watches = *il*	regard **e**	ils	regard **ent**	=	*they (masc. or mixed masc. and fem.) watch*
she/it watches = *elle*	regard **e**	elles	regard **ent**	=	*they (fem.) watch*
one watches = *on*	regard **e**				

IMPORTANT: 'il', 'elle' and 'on' always have the same ending, and so do 'ils' & 'elles'.

Endings for -ir verbs

To form the present tense of regular '-ir' verbs, add the endings shown to the verb's stem — e.g.:

The first bit ('fin') doesn't change. → *finir = to finish*

I finish	=	*je*	fin **is**	nous	fin **issons**	=	*we finish*
you (inf. sing.) finish	=	*tu*	fin **is**	vous	fin **issez**	=	*you (formal & plural) finish*
he/she/it/one finishes	=	*il/elle/on*	fin **it**	ils/elles	fin **issent**	=	*they finish*

Endings for -re verbs

To form the present tense of regular '-re' verbs, add the endings shown to the verb's stem — e.g.

The first bit ('vend') doesn't change. → *vendre = to sell*

I sell	=	*je*	vend **s**	*nous*	vend **ons**	=	*we sell*
you (inf. sing.) sell	=	*tu*	vend **s**	*vous*	vend **ez**	=	*you (formal & plural) sell*
he/she/it/one sells	=	*il/elle/on*	vend	*ils/elles*	vend **ent**	=	*they sell*

NOTE: For il/elle/on there's no ending for '-re' verbs.

The present tense — not just for Christmas...

You use the present tense for both 'I do something' and 'I am doing something'. Make sure you avoid disasters like 'Je suis... jouer... le tennis' for 'I am playing tennis'. Ouch. Roger Federer wouldn't say that, French-speaking Swiss pro that he is. He'd say 'Je joue au tennis'.

Verbs in the Present Tense

PRESENT TENSE

Verbs that don't follow the same pattern as regular verbs are called 'irregular verbs' (crazy, I know). Most of the really useful verbs are irregular — d'oh. Anyway, here are a few you'll need most...

Some of the most useful verbs are irregular

These are some of the most important verbs in the world, so you really must learn all the bits of them.

① *être* = to be

I am = *je* suis
you (informal singular) are = *tu* es
he/she/it/one is = *il/elle/on* est
we are = *nous* sommes
you (formal & plural) are = *vous* êtes
they are = *ils/elles* sont

② *avoir* = to have

I have = *j'*ai
you (informal singular) have = *tu* as
he/she/it/one has = *il/elle/on* a
we have = *nous* avons
you (formal & plural) have = *vous* avez
they have = *ils/elles* ont

③ *faire* = to make / to do

I make = *je* fais
you (informal singular) make = *tu* fais
he/she/it/one makes = *il/elle/on* fait
we make = *nous* faisons
you (formal & plural) make = *vous* faites
they make = *ils/elles* font

④ *aller* = to go

I go = *je* vais
you (informal singular) go = *tu* vas
he/she/it/one goes = *il/elle/on* va
we go = *nous* allons
you (formal & plural) go = *vous* allez
they go = *ils/elles* vont

⑤ *pouvoir* = to be able to / can

I can = *je* peux
you (informal singular) can = *tu* peux
he/she/it/one can = *il/elle/on* peut
we can = *nous* pouvons
you (formal & plural) can = *vous* pouvez
they can = *ils/elles* peuvent

⑥ *vouloir* = to want

I want = *je* veux
you (informal singular) want = *tu* veux
he/she/it/one wants = *il/elle/on* veut
we want = *nous* voulons
you (formal & plural) want = *vous* voulez
they want = *ils/elles* veulent

⑦ *devoir* = must / to have to

I must = *je* dois
you (informal singular) must = *tu* dois
he/she/it/one must = *il/elle/on* doit
we must = *nous* devons
you (formal & plural) must = *vous* devez
they must = *ils/elles* doivent

⑧ *savoir* = to know

I know = *je* sais
you (informal singular) know = *tu* sais
he/she/it/one knows = *il/elle/on* sait
we know = *nous* savons
you (formal & plural) know = *vous* savez
they know = *ils/elles* savent

To say 'we like eating', use 'we like to eat'

To say 'we like eating' you need two verbs. The first verb ('like') needs to be in the right form for the person. The second ('eat'), is just the infinitive.

swimming: nager *fishing:* pêcher *singing:* chanter

nous aimons manger = we like eating

Sometimes the first verb has a preposition — a small but important word that comes before the second verb:

il arrête de fumer = he is stopping smoking

je commence à parler = I start speaking

Irregular verbs — they should eat more fibre...

Don't worry, all these verb forms will become second nature eventually. The thing is that the irregular verbs tend to be the ones that are most used in French, so you can't just ignore them.

FUTURE TENSE

Talking About the Future

You'll need to talk about things that are going to happen at some point in the future and recognise when other people are talking about future events, too.

1) You can use 'I'm going to' to talk about the future

This is pretty easy, so there's no excuse for not learning it.

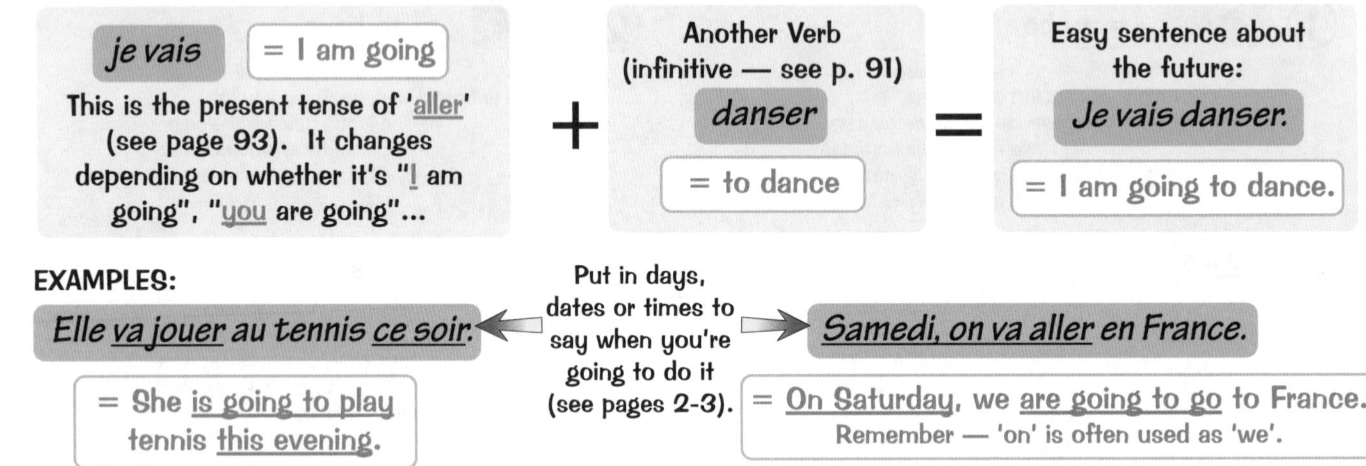

je vais
= I am going
This is the present tense of 'aller' (see page 93). It changes depending on whether it's "I am going", "you are going"...
+
Another Verb (infinitive — see p. 91)
danser
= to dance
=
Easy sentence about the future:
Je vais danser.
= I am going to dance.
EXAMPLES:
Elle va jouer au tennis ce soir.
= She is going to play tennis this evening.
Put in days, dates or times to say when you're going to do it (see pages 2-3).
Samedi, on va aller en France.
= On Saturday, we are going to go to France.
Remember — 'on' is often used as 'we'.

2) You have to recognise the Proper Future tense

The proper future tense in French is the equivalent of 'will' in English. You need to know what it means if you see it in the Reading or hear it in the Listening.

1) When -er and -ir verbs are in the future, you'll just see the infinitive (see page 91) + one of the following endings:

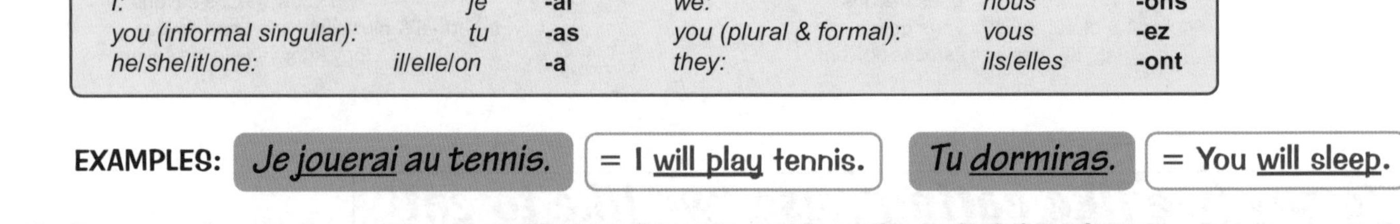

FUTURE TENSE ENDINGS

I:	*je*	**-ai**	*we:*	*nous*	**-ons**
you (informal singular):	*tu*	**-as**	*you (plural & formal):*	*vous*	**-ez**
he/she/it/one:	*il/elle/on*	**-a**	*they:*	*ils/elles*	**-ont**

2) For -re verbs, it's the same, except the 'e' will be missing from the end of the infinitive.

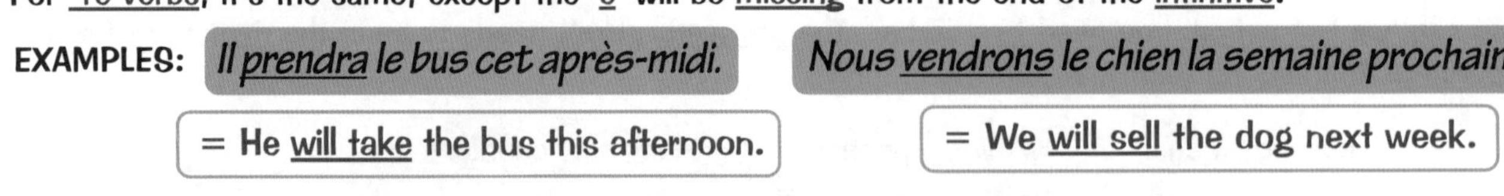

EXAMPLES:
Il prendra le bus cet après-midi.
= He will take the bus this afternoon.
Nous vendrons le chien la semaine prochaine.
= We will sell the dog next week.

3) The verbs below don't follow the pattern — they have the same endings, but different stems.

VERB	STEM	VERB	STEM	VERB	STEM	VERB	STEM
faire	fer-	*aller*	ir-	*avoir*	aur-	*être*	ser-
vouloir	voudr-	*pouvoir*	pourr-	*venir*	viendr-	*devoir*	devr-

I'm going to go insane...

Spend a good chunk of time mastering that aller + infinitive stuff — it can really spice up what you say or write in your assessments. When you've got to grips with that, move on to the proper future tense — make sure you'll be able to spot future verbs a mile off — and learn those irregulars, too...

Talking About the Past

PERFECT TENSE

The perfect tense is used for things that happened in the past. It's a bit tricky so we've given you three pages on it. Like most grammar stuff, it's just a question of a few rules to follow, and a few bits and pieces to learn. Nothing you can't handle, I'm sure.

Qu'est-ce que tu as fait? — What have you done?

You have to be able to make and understand sentences like this:

There are two important bits: *J'ai joué au tennis.* = I (have) played tennis.

1) You always need a bit to mean 'I have' (more on the next page). In English, you don't always need the 'have', like in 'last week, I played tennis'. BUT in French you have to have the 'have'.

2) This bit means 'played'. It's a special version of 'jouer' (to play). In English, most of these words end in '-ed'. See below.

I have played: for 'have' use 'avoir'

For the 'have' bit of these past tense phrases, you use the present tense of 'avoir:'

EXAMPLES

Tu as joué au tennis. = You have played tennis.

Elle a joué au tennis. = She has played tennis.

Nous avons joué au tennis. = We have played tennis.

AVOIR = TO HAVE

I have =	j'ai
you (informal singular) have =	tu as
he/she/it/one has =	il/elle/on a
we have =	nous avons
you (formal & plural) have =	vous avez
they have =	ils/elles ont

Joué = played: these are Past Participles

The past participle is the bit of the verb which usually ends -ed in English, for example played, climbed, laughed. In French, regular verbs form their past participles like this:

-ER VERBS

FORMULA

Remove '-er', then add 'é'

EXAMPLES

jouer — joué
to play played
aller — allé
to go gone

-IR VERBS

FORMULA

Remove '-r'

EXAMPLES

partir — parti
to leave left
choisir — choisi
to choose chosen

-RE VERBS

FORMULA

Remove '-re', then add 'u'

EXAMPLES

vendre — vendu
to sell sold
attendre — attendu
to wait waited

That's all perfectly clear...

This page might look pretty complicated, but don't let it overwhelm you — if you know the present tense of avoir inside out and you learn how regular past participles are formed then you'll be well on the way to understanding the basics of the perfect tense. Only two more pages to go...

PERFECT TENSE

Talking About the Past

So you've met the regular verbs in the perfect tense, now for the irregular verbs. And sadly, there are quite a few of them.

Lots of verbs have irregular past participles

Some verbs don't follow the patterns. It's dead annoying, because a lot of the most useful verbs are irregular — you just have to learn them by heart:

Verb	Past Participle	Translation
avoir:	eu	*had*
boire:	bu	*drank / drunk*
conduire:	conduit	*drove / driven*
connaître:	connu	*knew / known*
courir:	couru	*ran / run*
devoir:	dû	*had to*
dire:	dit	*said*
écrire:	écrit	*wrote*
être:	été	*was*
faire:	fait	*did*

Verb	Past Participle	Translation
lire:	lu	*read*
mettre:	mis	*put*
ouvrir:	ouvert	*opened*
pouvoir:	pu	*was able / been able*
prendre:	pris	*took / taken*
rire:	ri	*laughed*
savoir:	su	*knew / known*
voir:	vu	*saw / seen*
vouloir:	voulu	*wanted*

Make sure you really get to grips with the perfect tense

The key to doing well in French GCSE is using a variety of different tenses, so being able to talk about the past is really important. There's one more page of stuff on the perfect tense to go, but it's worth having a good look at these example sentences and really getting your head round them before you move on.

J'ai mangé dans un restaurant. = I have eaten / I ate in a restaurant.

Tu as mangé dans un restaurant. = You have eaten / you ate in a restaurant.

Il a mangé dans un restaurant. = He has eaten / he ate in a restaurant.

This would be almost exactly the same if you were talking about a girl except that 'il' would change to 'elle'.

Nous avons mangé dans un restaurant. = We have eaten / we ate in a restaurant.

Vous avez mangé dans un restaurant. = You have eaten / ate in a restaurant.

Ils ont mangé dans un restaurant. = They (masc.) have eaten / ate in a restaurant.

This would be almost exactly the same if you were talking about girls except that 'ils' would change to 'elles'.

Bet you're perfectly tense by now...

I know it seems like there's a lot to learn for just one tense, but I promise you that the time you spend learning this won't be wasted. It always comes up and it really is the key to doing well.

Talking About the Past

Perfect Tense

One last thing — there are a handful of verbs which don't use 'avoir' at all in the perfect tense...

A few verbs use être instead of avoir

1) A small number of verbs use the present tense of 'être' instead of the present tense of avoir when forming the perfect tense.
2) Just like with verbs that take 'avoir,' you use the bit of 'être' that matches the person you're talking about. E.g. He went = Il est allé.
3) The only difference with verbs that take être is that the past participle has to agree with the person its describing. More on this below.

ÊTRE = TO BE

I am =	je suis
you (informal singular) are =	tu es
he/she/it/one is =	il/elle/on est
we are =	nous sommes
you (formal & plural) are =	vous êtes
they are =	ils/elles sont

There are 15 exceptions — learn them

Verb	Past Participle	Translation
aller:	allé	went /gone
rester:	resté	stayed
venir:	venu	came /come
devenir:	devenu	became / become
arriver:	arrivé	arrived
partir:	parti	left
sortir:	sorti	went out / gone out
entrer:	entré	entered
monter:	monté	went up / gone up
descendre:	descendu	went down / gone down

Verb	Past Participle	Translation
rentrer:	rentré	went back / gone back
retourner:	retourné	returned
tomber:	tombé	fell / fallen
naître:	né	was born / been born
mourir:	mort	died

The être verbs are mostly about movement, being born or dying. You also have to use être with reflexive verbs — see page 99.

EXAMPLES:

See below for why this 'e' is there.

Je suis allé(e) au cinéma. = I have gone to the cinema.

Il est arrivé. = He has arrived.

With être as the auxiliary verb, the past participle must agree

When you use être to form the perfect tense, the past participle has to agree with the subject of the verb. This means it changes if the subject is feminine or plural, just like an adjective (see page 80). The agreements are underlined:

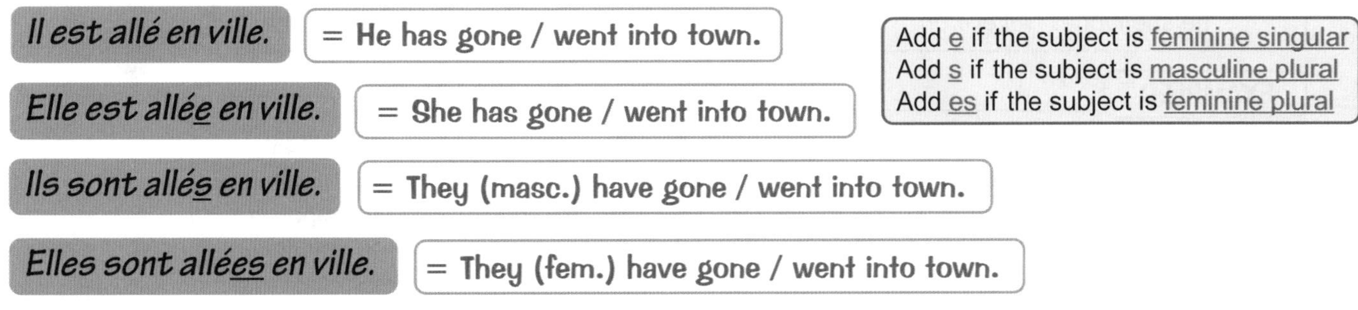

Il est allé en ville. = He has gone / went into town.

Elle est allée en ville. = She has gone / went into town.

Ils sont allés en ville. = They (masc.) have gone / went into town.

Elles sont allées en ville. = They (fem.) have gone / went into town.

Add e if the subject is feminine singular
Add s if the subject is masculine plural
Add es if the subject is feminine plural

The 15 exceptions that prove the rule...

So, not only are loads and loads of the past participles irregular, you can't even be sure that the verb you want to put in the perfect takes 'avoir'. Except you can — by learning which ones don't.

Imperfect Tense

'Was Doing' or 'Used to Do'

Another past tense for you. This one's used for describing what was going on, setting the scene and talking about what you used to do.

Être, avoir and faire crop up a lot

These are the only three verbs you need to use in the imperfect, so make sure you learn them inside out.

ÊTRE = TO BE

j'étais:	I was
tu étais:	you *(informal sing.)* were
il/elle/on était:	he/she/it/one was
nous étions:	we were
vous étiez:	you (formal & pl.) were
ils/elles étaient:	they were

Vous étiez très petit = You were very small

Ce roman était magnifique = This novel was great

And of course... *C'était...* = It was...

AVOIR = TO HAVE

j'avais:	I was having
tu avais:	you *(informal sing.)* were having
il/elle/on avait:	he/she/it/one was having
nous avions:	we were having
vous aviez:	you (*formal & pl.*) were having
ils/elles avaient:	they were having

Il y avait deux pizzas = There were two pizzas

Tu avais trois chiens = You used to have three dogs

J'avais une caravane = I used to have a caravan

FAIRE = TO DO

je faisais:	I was doing
tu faisais:	you *(informal sing.)* were doing
il/elle/on faisait:	he/she/it/one was doing
nous faisions:	we were doing
vous faisiez:	you (*formal & pl.*) were doing
ils/elles faisaient:	they were doing

Il faisait beau = The weather was nice

Ils faisaient des courses = They were shopping

Nous faisions nos devoirs = We were doing our homework

Learn to recognise Imperfect endings

As well as knowing how to use 'avoir', 'être' and 'faire' in the imperfect, you need to recognise the imperfect forms of other common French verbs. Luckily, it's easy to spot — it's just the present tense 'nous' form of the verb (see p.92-93) with its -ons ending removed and replaced by one of these imperfect endings:

IMPERFECT TENSE ENDINGS

I:	*je*	**-ais**	we:	*nous*	**-ions**
you (informal sing.):	*tu*	**-ais**	you (plu. & formal):	*vous*	**-iez**
he/she/it/one:	*il/elle/on*	**-ait**	they:	*ils/elles*	**-aient**

I used to have a life

EXAMPLES

In English	In French	In English	In French
I was wanting	je voulais	They (masc.) were knowing	ils savaient
He was speaking	il parlait	You (pl.) were able to	vous pouviez
We were going	nous allions	You (sing.) were coming	tu venais

Once upon a time, there was a lovely tense...

Not a bad page — apart from the stuff you have to recognise, there are only three verbs to learn. Make sure you do conquer être, avoir and faire though — you'll use them more than you reckon.

Myself, Yourself, etc.

Reflexive Verbs

Sometimes you have to talk about things you do to yourself — like washing yourself or getting yourself up in the morning.

Talking about yourself — me, te, se...

Here are all the different ways to say 'self':

You can tell which verbs need 'self' by checking in the dictionary. If you look up 'to get up', it'll say 'se lever'.

myself:	me	*ourselves:*	nous
yourself (informal):	te	*yourself (formal), yourselves:*	vous
himself:	se	*themselves, each other:*	se
herself:	se		
oneself:	se		

Je me leve — I get up

You need to be able to talk about your 'daily morning routine' (what you do when you get up), and other things which are about what you do to yourself.

SE LEVER = TO GET UP

I get (myself) up:	je me lève	*one gets (oneself) up:*	on se lève
you get (yourself) up (informal):	tu te lèves	*we get (ourselves) up:*	nous nous levons
he gets (himself) up:	il se lève	*you get (yourself (formal) / yourselves) up:*	vous vous levez
she gets (herself) up:	elle se lève	*they get (themselves) up:*	ils/elles se lèvent

There are lots of these verbs, but here are the ones you should know for the exams. Learn these:

THE 8 IMPORTANT REFLEXIVE VERBS

to enjoy oneself:	s'amuser	Il s'amuse:	*He's enjoying himself.*
to go to bed:	se coucher	Je me couche à onze heures:	*I go to bed at 11 o'clock.*
to wash oneself:	se laver	Je me lave le soir:	*I wash myself in the evening.*
to feel:	se sentir	Tu te sens mal?:	*Do you feel ill?*
to be called (literally = to call oneself):	s'appeler	Je m'appelle Bob:	*I'm called Bob. (literally = I call myself Bob)*
to excuse oneself / to be sorry / to apologise:	s'excuser	Je m'excuse...:	*I'm sorry / I apologise.*
to be (literally = to find oneself):	se trouver	Où se trouve la banque?:	*Where is the bank? (literally = Where does the bank find itself?)*
to be interested in:	s'intéresser à	Je m'intéresse au tennis:	*I'm interested in tennis.*

Je me suis levé(e) — I got up

1) The perfect tense (see p.95-97) of these verbs is pretty much the same as normal except they all go with 'être', not 'avoir'. The only tricky bit is working out where to put the 'me' or 'te' or 'se' or whatever — and it goes right after the 'je', 'tu' or 'il' etc. (In other words, it's before the bit of 'être'.)

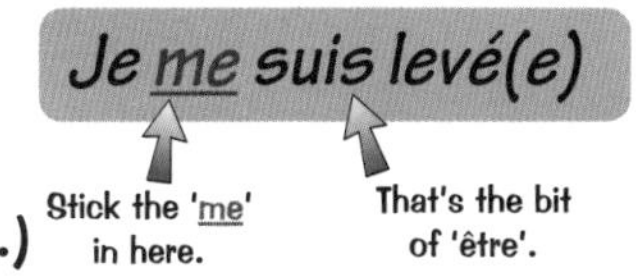

2) Like other verbs which use 'être' for the perfect tense, you might have to add on an 'e' and/or an 's', to match who's doing it. If you're female, make sure you add an 'e' when you're talking about yourself.

EXAMPLES:

- *Je me suis levée.* = I (fem.) got up.
- *Elle s'est levée.* = She got up.
- *Ils se sont levés.* = They (masc. or mixed gender) got up.
- *Elles se sont levées.* = They (fem.) got up.

Reflexive verbs are really common in French...

...even when it's not obvious that someone's doing something to themselves. Try writing down a few sentences with reflexive verbs — some in the present and some in the perfect tense. Do it NOW.

NEGATIVES — How to Say 'Not', 'Never' & 'Nothing'

This stuff's easy enough. Well, most of it is...

Use 'ne ... pas' to say not

1) In English you change a sentence to mean the opposite by adding 'not'.
2) In French, you have to add two little words, 'ne' and 'pas'. They go either side of the verb (see p.91).

Je suis Bob. (= I am Bob.) → Je ne suis pas Bob. (= I am not Bob.)

This is the verb. The 'ne' goes in front, and the 'pas' goes after.

3) For verbs in the perfect tense (see p.95-97), you stick the 'ne' and 'pas' around the bit of avoir or être.

Je n'ai pas vu ça. (= I have not seen that.) Elle n'est pas arrivée. (= She has not arrived.)

For an infinitive, the ne and pas go together

The 'ne' and 'pas' usually go either side of the action word (the verb).
BUT if the action word is an infinitive (see page 91) then the 'ne' and the 'pas' both go in front of it.

Je préfère voir un film. (= I prefer to see a film.) → Je préfère ne pas voir un film. (= I prefer not to see a film.)

ne ... jamais — never ne ... rien — nothing

There are more negatives you need to understand, and to really impress you should use them too.

Je ne vais jamais à York. = I never go to York. (I don't ever go to York.)

Je ne vais ni à York ni à Belfast. = I neither go to York nor to Belfast.

Je ne vais plus à Belfast. = I no longer go to Belfast. (I don't go to Belfast any more.)

not ever (never): ne ... jamais
neither ... nor: ne ... ni ... ni
no longer (any more): ne plus
not anybody (nobody): ne ... personne
not anything (nothing): ne ... rien

Il n'y a personne ici. = There isn't anybody here. (There is nobody here.)

Il n'y a rien ici. = There isn't anything here. (There is nothing here.)

Je n'ai pas de... — I don't have any...

After a negative, articles such as 'un/une', 'du', 'de la' or 'des' are always replaced by just 'de'.

Je n'ai pas d'argent. (= I haven't got any money.)

Elle n'a plus de chocolat. (= She hasn't got any more chocolate.)

The 'de' is only shortened if the next word begins with a vowel or an 'h' which takes 'l''. E.g. 'd'argent', 'd'animaux'.

Just say no — & nobody & nothing & never & not...

OK, just one more thing, then I'll be quiet. When you want 'nobody' or 'nothing' to be the subject of the sentence, you have to say "Personne ne..." or "Rien ne...". E.g. "Personne ne nous a vus" = "Nobody saw us", and "Rien ne s'est passé" = "Nothing happened" (se passer = to happen).

Ordering People Around

IMPERATIVE

Ordering people around — the quicker you learn it, the quicker you can get on with your life...

You need this for bossing people about

It looks like the present tense (see p.92) but without the 'tu', 'vous' or 'nous' bits.

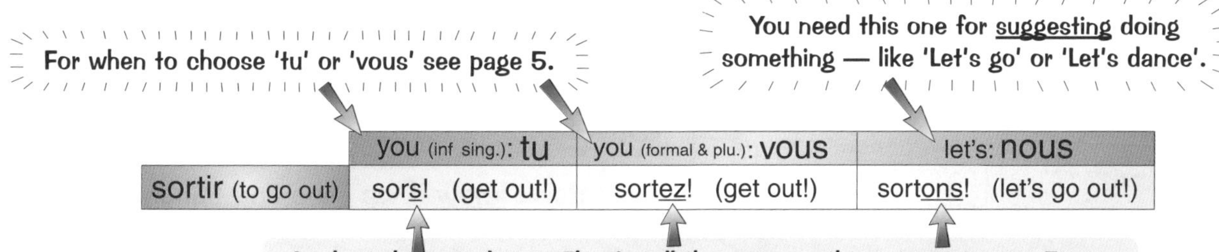
For when to choose 'tu' or 'vous' see page 5.
You need this one for suggesting doing something — like 'Let's go' or 'Let's dance'.

	you (inf sing.): tu	you (formal & plu.): vous	let's: nous
sortir (to go out)	sors! (get out!)	sortez! (get out!)	sortons! (let's go out!)

Look at these endings. They're all the same as the present tense. Easy.

EXAMPLES

Vendons la voiture! = Let's sell the car!

Écoute ça! = Listen to that!

Finissez vos devoirs! = Finish your homework!

Whip off the 's' from the 'tu' form of '-er' verbs

The odd one out is any 'tu' form that ends in 'es'. That means you have to be careful with regular -er verbs. You just have to lose the final '-s':

Regarde Jean-Paul! = Look at Jean-Paul!

Arrête de m'énerver! = Stop annoying me!

The ones below are irregular. They're nothing like the present tense, so you have to learn them by heart.

	you (inf. sing.): tu	you (formal & plu.): vous	let's: nous
to be: être	sois (be)	soyez (be)	soyons (let's be)
to have: avoir	aie (have)	ayez (have)	ayons (let's have)
to know: savoir	sache (know)	sachez (know)	sachons (let's know)

Negatives work normally, except for reflexives

Put 'ne' in front of the verb and 'pas' after, like normal (see page 100). Add the noun at the end.

EXAMPLES: *N'écoute pas!* = Don't listen! *Ne vendez pas la voiture!* = Don't sell the car!

In sentences with a reflexive verb (see p.99) you have to use an emphatic pronoun (p.87), and fiddle the word order...

E.g. *Tu te lèves.* = You get up. ➡ *Lève-toi!* = Get up!

WATCH OUT though — in negative sentences, you use normal pronouns and normal word order.

E.g. *Tu ne te lèves pas.* = You don't get up. ➡ *Ne te lève pas!* = Don't get up!

If it's imperative, it must be important...

Hopefully you haven't found this too horrendous. But do be careful about dropping the 's' from the 'tu' form of '-er' verbs — that catches out many a weary traveller. Oh, and negatives aren't obvious, so take another look at those before you whizz on to the next page.

Savoir, Connaître and Pouvoir

Know and Can

Sooo many people get these verbs confused — so learn them right now.

'To know information' is 'Savoir'

1) Savoir means 'to know' in the sense of knowing information (e.g. knowing what time the bus leaves).

DIFFERENT FORMS OF SAVOIR

I know	je sais
you (informal singular) know	tu sais
he/she/it/one knows	il/elle/on sait
we know	nous savons
you (formal and plural) know	vous savez
they know	ils/elles savent

Elle sait la réponse. = She knows the answer.

Je ne sais pas si nous avons des bananes. = I don't know if we have any bananas.

2) Savoir followed by an infinitive means 'to know how to do something', in the sense of a skill...

EXAMPLES: *Je sais conduire.* = I can drive. *Elle ne sait pas lire.* = She can't read.

'To be familiar with' is 'Connaître'

Connaître means to know a person or place — to 'be familiar with'.
If someone asks you whether you know their mate Bob, this is the one to use.

DIFFERENT FORMS OF CONNAÎTRE

I know	je connais
you (informal singular) know	tu connais
he/she/it/one knows	il/elle/on connaît
we know	nous connaissons
you (formal and plural) know	vous connaissez
they know	ils/elles connaissent

Connais-tu mon ami? = Do you know my friend?

Je connais bien Paris. = I know Paris well.

'Pouvoir' — to be able to

Pouvoir (to be able to/can) has three very important meanings:

1) Being able to do something (not knowing how, but just being able — like 'Yes, I can come tomorrow').

Je peux porter les bagages, si tu veux. = I can carry the luggage, if you like.

Elle ne peut pas venir ce matin. = She cannot come this morning.

2) Permission to do something. *On peut prendre des photos ici.* = You can take photos here.

Tu ne peux pas rester demain. = You can't stay tomorrow.

3) Possibility — something could or might be the case.

Cela peut arriver. = That can happen.

DIFFERENT FORMS OF POUVOIR

I can	je peux
you (informal singular) can	tu peux
he/she/it/one can	il/elle/on peut
we can	nous pouvons
you (formal and plural) can	vous pouvez
they can	ils/elles peuvent

When the can-can's a know-know...

Easy question: how do you say, "I can speak French" in French? "Je peux parler français"? Wrong — it's "Je sais parler français". French is a skill you've learned, so it takes 'savoir'.

'Had Done' and 'Would'

PLUPERFECT TENSE & CONDITIONAL

Two more bits to learn — keep at it, the grammar section's nearly over...

J'avais fait — I had done

1) The pluperfect is like the perfect tense (see p.95-97) — that's for saying what you have done, but this is for saying what you had done. You only have to recognise it.
2) It's still made up of a bit of avoir or être + a past participle but the bit of avoir or être is in the imperfect tense.
3) For verbs that take être, don't forget to check the ending of the past participle to see if it's referring to something masculine or feminine.

For stuff on the imperfect tense, see page 98.

RECOGNISING THE PLUPERFECT

IMPERFECT TENSE OF AVOIR / ÊTRE + PAST PARTICIPLE

J'avais écrit une lettre à mon père. = I had written a letter to my father.

Nous étions allés voir un film au cinéma. = We had gone to see a film at the cinema.

Betty et Sarah étaient arrivées. = Betty and Sarah had arrived.

Je voudrais voir un film — I'd like to see a film

The conditional translates as 'would do something'. These two verbs are the only ones you need to know in the conditional, and you've been using 'je voudrais' for years, so it should be easy to get right:

① **VOULOIR**

I would like:	je voudrais
you (informal singular) would like:	tu voudrais
he/she/it/one would like:	il/elle/on voudrait
we would like:	nous voudrions
you (formal & plural) would like:	vous voudriez
they would like:	ils/elles voudraient

Je voudrais aller à l'hôpital. = I would like to go to hospital.

Je voudrais de la glace. = I would like some ice cream

Even though 'vouloir' usually means 'to want', in the conditional it's translated as 'would like'.

② **AIMER**

I would like:	j'aimerais
you (informal singular) would like:	tu aimerais
he/she/it/one would like:	il/elle/on aimerait
we would like:	nous aimerions
you (formal & plural) would like:	vous aimeriez
they would like:	ils/elles aimeraient

J'aimerais du lait. = I would like some milk.

J'aimerais sortir. = I would like to go out.

I would like the next page to be the last...

You're in luck. All apart from that pesky revision summary, the next page is the last thing you'll have to learn for GCSE French. Provided you didn't start learning from the back, that is...

IMPERSONAL VERBS, THE PASSIVE & PRESENT PARTICIPLES

'Il faut,' the Passive and '-ing'

Some pretty meaty stuff on this page. But don't despair — one final push and you'll have finished the grammar section.

Impersonal verbs only work with 'il'

Impersonal verbs always have 'il' as the subject. This means you translate them as 'it is'. For example:

Il faut aller au collège tous les jours. = It is necessary to go to school every day.

ANOTHER EXAMPLE:

Il faut manger le petit déjeuner le matin. = It is necessary to eat breakfast in the morning.

La tasse est cassée — The cup is broken

1) In most sentences, there's a person or thing doing the action that's described by the verb. In a passive sentence, the person or thing is having something done to it.
2) The passive in French is made up of a person or thing + être + past participle. You just have to recognise the present tense form of the passive.
3) The past participle has to agree with the person or thing that is having the action done to it.

Elle est choisie par le prof. = She is chosen by the teacher.

'est' is a present tense form of the verb 'être' — to see the rest of it in the present, go to page 93.

See p.95-97 for more past participles.

ANOTHER EXAMPLE:

Les biscuits sont mangés par le cheval. = The biscuits are eaten by the horse.

Words that end in -ant are present participles

1) The present participle is the equivalent of the English '-ing' ending.
2) In French, it doesn't mean 'I am doing' like in English. Those kind of sentences use the present tense (see pages 92-93) instead.
3) French present participles are made up of the imperfect stem of the verb + -ant. You might see it being used as an adjective, which means it agrees if it's talking about a feminine or plural thing (see p.80-82):

L'enfant pleurant. = The crying child. *La fille pleurante.* = The crying girl.

Fi fie faut fum — it seems to me the book is done...

You are indeed very near the end now, but you do need to fully understand the stuff on this page before you move on to the revision summary, especially the stuff about 'il faut,' which'll make you sound really French. For the last time — get some paper, cover up the page and get scribbling...

Revision Summary

EVERYTHING IMPORTANT

It's the last time you'll see the shocking words above — words that spread fear and loathing across the nation. That's right, this is the final French 'Revision Summary'. Whoop whoop.

1) Give the words for both '<u>the</u>' and '<u>a</u>' (where appropriate) which have to accompany these:
a) maison b) chien c) chaussure d) soleil e) travail f) jeu g) jeux h) journaux

2) Je vais à la maison... Change this sentence to tell people you're going to:
a) le cinéma b) l'église c) la banque d) le stade e) les magasins f) les Alpes

3) How would you say in French: a) the pink dress b) the big bird c) the brand new car

4) What are the French words for: a) my horse b) our house c) his clothes d) her house

5) And the French for: a) You (pl.) talk weirdly. b) They (fem.) dance slowly.

6) "Janie is cool. Janie is cooler than Jimmy. Janie is the coolest." Translate these three sentences into French, then swap "cool" for each of the following words and write them out all over again:
a) formidable b) intelligent(e) c) célèbre d) pratique e) bavard(e)

7) Write a French sentence for each of the following French words. Then put them all together ... et voilà... you have your very own (probably weird) French poem.
a) à b) en c) dans d) pour e) depuis f) de g) en face de

8) Translate the following text:
J'ai rencontré un homme qui adorait les sports. Cet homme que j'ai rencontré, qui adorait les sports, n'aimait pas les champignons que je lui avais achetés.

9) Give the French words for:
a) and b) or c) but d) because e) with

10) Write down the following in French:
a) I have b) she has c) we have d) they have e) I am f) he is g) we are h) they are

11) What do each of these French phrases mean in English:
a) Je fais un gâteau b) J'ai fait un gâteau c) Je faisais un gâteau
d) J'avais fait un gâteau e) Je vais faire un gâteau f) Je ferai un gâteau

12) Sadly, growing up means learning to do things for yourself. Using reflexive verbs, say:
a) We get up. b) She went to bed. c) They apologised. d) I'm interested in French.

13) Ah, negativity. We'll have none of that here. Well, apart from these phrases.
Say these three in French: a) I don't go out. b) I never go out. c) Nobody goes out.

14) Going commando. Turn these sentences from the present tense to the imperative.
a) Tu arrêtes de faire ça. b) Vous êtes tranquil.
c) Nous allons au Portugal. d) Tu te lèves. e) Nous ne regardons pas le film.

15) Translate: a) Nous étions allées au pays de Galles.
b) Il faut manger beaucoup de légumes.
c) Le gâteau est mangé par moi.

Do Well in Your Exam

Here are some little gems of advice, whichever exam board you're studying for.

Read the Questions carefully

Don't go losing easy marks — it'll break my heart.
Make sure you definitely do the things on this list:

1) Read all the instructions properly.
2) Read the question properly.
3) Answer the question — don't waffle.

Don't give up if you don't Understand

If you don't understand, don't panic. The key thing to remember is that you can still do well in the exam, even if you don't understand every French word that comes up. Just use one of the two methods below:

If you're reading or listening — look for lookalikes

1) Some words look or sound the same in French and English — they're called cognates.
2) These words are great because you'll recognise them when you see them in a text.
3) Be careful though — there are some exceptions you need to watch out for. Some words look like an English word but have a totally different meaning:

grand(e):	*big /tall*	la pièce:	*room, coin or play*	les affaires:	*business, stuff*
large:	*wide*	la veste:	*jacket*	le pain:	*bread*
mince:	*slim*	le médecin:	*doctor*	les baskets:	*trainers*
joli(e):	*pretty*	le car:	*coach*	la location:	*rental*
la journée:	*day*	le crayon:	*pencil*		

Words like these are called 'faux amis' — false friends.

Use your Common Sense

You'll likely come across the odd word that you don't know, especially in the reading exam. Often you'll be able to find some clues telling you what the text is all about.

1) The type of text, e.g. newspaper article, advertisement, website
2) The title of the text
3) Any pictures
4) The verbal context

Say you see the following in the reading exam, and don't know what any of these words mean:

"...des vêtements en polyester, en soie, en laine et en coton."

1) Well, the fact that this is a list of things, all starting with 'en ...' coming after the French word for 'clothes' suggests they're all things that clothes can be made out of.
2) You can guess that 'polyester' means 'polyester', and 'coton' means 'cotton'.
3) So it's a pretty good guess that the two words you don't know are different types of fabric. (In fact, 'soie' means 'silk' and 'laine' means 'wool'.)
4) Most questions won't depend on you understanding these more difficult words. It's important to be able to understand the gist though, and not let these words throw you.

Friend or faux...

Don't get caught out by words that look like English words, but in fact mean something different. Generally speaking, if a word doesn't seem to fit into the context of the question, have a re-think.

Do Well in Your Exam

These pages could improve your grade — they're all about exam technique. No learning in sight...

Look at how a word is made up

You may read or hear a sentence and not understand how the sentence works. You need to remember all the grammary bits in section 7 to give you a good chance at piecing it all together.

1) A word that ends in '-é', '-u' or '-i' may well be a past participle. Look for a bit of 'avoir' or a bit of 'être' nearby to work out who's done what.
2) A word that ends in 'r' or 'er' might be an infinitive. If you take off the 'er', it might look like an English word which may tell you what the verb means.

   E.g. 'confirm~~er~~' = to confirm

3) If you see '-ment' at the end of a word, it could well be an adverb (see page 83). Try replacing the '-ment' with '-ly' and see if it makes sense.

   E.g. 'générale~~ment~~' ➔ 'généralely' = generally

4) 'Dés-' at the beginning of a word is often 'dis-' in the equivalent word in English.

   E.g. 'd~~é~~savantage' = disadvantage

5) Sometimes letters with accents show that there may have been an 's' at some point in the past. This may help you find the corresponding English word.

   E.g. 'tempête' = tempest 'hôpital' = hospital 'forêt' = forest

6) A word beginning with 'in-' might be a negative prefix.

   E.g. 'l'inconvénient' = 'in+convénient' = inconvenience

A prefix is a part of a word that comes before the main bit of the word.

Take notes in the listening exam

1) You'll have 5 minutes at the start of the exam to have a quick look through the paper. This'll give you a chance to see how many questions there are, and you might get a few clues from the questions about what topics they're on, so it won't be a horrible surprise when the tape starts running.
2) You'll hear each extract twice. Different people have different strategies, but it's a good idea to jot down a few details that you think might come up in the questions, especially things like:
3) But... don't forget to keep listening to the recording while you're making notes.
4) You won't have a dictionary — but you probably wouldn't have time to use it anyway.

Dates
Numbers
Spelled-out names

Look at how to make words up — no, wait...

The examiners aren't above sticking a few tricky bits and pieces into the exam to see how you cope with them. Using all your expert knowledge, you should stand a pretty good chance of working it out. And if you can't make an educated guess, make an uneducated guess... but try something.

How To Use Dictionaries

Don't go mad on dictionaries — it's the path to ruin. However, you're allowed to use one in the writing task, so it's good to know how to make the most of it.

Don't translate Word for Word — it DOESN'T work

If you turn each word of this phrase into English, you get rubbish.

Il y a une pomme. → *It there has an apple.*

NO!

I am reading. → *Je suis lisant.*

It's the same the other way round — turn English into French word by word, and you get balderdash — don't do it.

If it Doesn't make Sense, you've got it Wrong

Some words have several meanings — don't just pick the first one you see. Look at the meanings listed and suss out which one is what you're looking for.

If you read this... *J'ai mal à l'oeil droit.*

...you might look up 'droit' and find this:

> **droit, e**
> adj upright; straight;
> // right, right-hand
> // adv straight //
> tiens-toi droit: stand up straight
> // nm law; justice
> // droits; rights; taxes, duties
> droits d'auteur: royalties

So the sentence could mean:

- *My straight eye hurts.* ✗
- *My right eye hurts.* ✓
- *My law eye hurts.* ✗

This is the only one that sounds sensible.

Verbs change according to the person

When you look up a verb in the dictionary, you'll find the infinitive (the 'to' form, like 'to run', 'to sing' etc.). But you may need to say 'I run', or 'we sing' — so you need to change the verb ending.

Say you need to say 'I work'.

1) If you looked up 'work', you'd find the word 'travailler', meaning 'to work'.
2) But 'travailler' is the infinitive — you can't put 'je travailler'.
3) You need the 'I' (je) form of the verb — 'je travaille'.
4) Check the tense too — you might want e.g. 'j'ai travaillé'.

For the low-down on verbs and all their different endings, see the grammar section.

If you're looking up a French verb, look for its infinitive (it'll end in 'er', 'ir' or 're'). If you want to know what 'nous cherchons' means, you'll find 'chercher' (to search, or to look for) in the dictionary. So 'nous cherchons' must mean 'we search' or 'we look for'.

Dictionaries — useful for holding doors open*...

Don't get put off dictionaries by this page. They're lovely really. Just make sure your writing technique isn't to look up every single word and then bung them down in order. Cos it'll be rubbish.

* No. 37 from a list of '101 great uses for your dictionary'.

Hints for Writing

Here are a few general hints about how you should approach the writing tasks.

Write about what you know

1) You won't be asked to write about complicated issues like world peace.
2) You will need to cover certain specific things that the question asks you to, but there'll be plenty of scope to be imaginative.
3) Usually the writing tasks will give you some flexibility so you can base your answer on something you know about.

Examiners like to know When and Why...

So, if I add one more drop we'll go back in time two hours...

...two hours later...

1) Saying when and how often you did things gets you big bonus marks. Learn times, dates and numbers carefully (pages 1-3).
2) Make sure you talk about what you've done in the past (see pages 95-98) or what you will do in the future (page 94).
3) Give descriptions where possible, but keep things accurate — a short description in perfect French is better than a longer paragraph of nonsense.
4) Examiners also love opinions (pages 7-8). Try to vary them as much as possible.

...and Where and Who With...

The examiners really are quite nosy, and love as many details as you can give. It's a good idea to ask yourself all these 'wh-' questions, and write the bits that show your French off in the best light. Also, it doesn't matter if what you're writing is strictly true — as long as it's believable.

Use your dictionary, but not too much

1) The time to use the dictionary is NOT to learn a completely new, fancy way of saying something.
2) Use it to look up a particular word that you've forgotten — a word that, when you see it, you'll know it's the right word.
3) Use it to check genders of nouns — that's whether words are masculine (le/un) or feminine (la/une).
4) Check any spellings you're unsure of.

Most importantly, don't use the dictionary to look for completely new words. If you don't know what you've written is right, it's probably wrong.

Take your time

Take me.

1) Don't hurtle into writing about something and then realise half-way through that you don't actually know the French for it.
2) Plan how you can cover all the things that the task mentions, and then think about the extra things you can slip in to show off your French.

And lastly, don't forget your pen...

I suppose the key is variety — lots of different tenses, plenty of meaty vocabulary and loads of details. This is your only chance to show what you can do, so don't waste all your hard work.

Hints for Writing

Accuracy is really important in the writing assessment. Without it, your work will look like sloppy custard.

Start with the Verb

Verbs are doing words.
See page 91.

1) Verbs really are the cornerstone of every French sentence.
   If you get the verb right, the rest of the sentence should fall into place.
2) Be careful that you get the whole expression that uses the verb, not just the verb itself.

EXAMPLE: Say you want to write the following sentence in French:

On Sundays, we go for a walk.

Don't see 'go' and jump in with 'aller'.
The expression for 'go for a walk' is 'faire une promenade'.

Make sure your tenses and the endings of the verbs are right, then piece it all together:

Le dimanche, nous faisons une promenade.

Check and re-check

No matter how careful you think you're being, mistakes can easily creep into your work.
Go through the check-list below for every sentence straight after you've written it.

1) Are the verbs in the right TENSE?
   Hier, je travaille dans le jardin. ✗ — Hier, j'ai travaillé dans le jardin. ✓
2) Are the ENDINGS of the verbs right?
   Tu n'aime pas les carottes? ✗ — Tu n'aimes pas les carottes? ✓
3) Do your adjectives AGREE as they should?
   Elle est grand. ✗ — Elle est grande. ✓
4) Do your past participles AGREE?
   Ils sont parti. ✗ — Ils sont partis. ✓
5) Do your adjectives come in the RIGHT PLACE?
   Une rose chemise ✗ — Une chemise rose ✓
6) Have you used TU / VOUS correctly?
   Monsieur, peux-tu m'aider, s'il vous plaît? ✗ — Monsieur, pouvez-vous m'aider, s'il vous plaît? ✓

Then when you've finished the whole piece of work, have another read through with fresh eyes.
You're bound to pick up one or two more mistakes.

Do nothing without a verb...

I know there's loads to remember, and French verbs are a pain, but checking over your work is a real must. Re-read your work assuming there are errors in it, rather than assuming it's fine as it is.

Hints for Speaking

The speaking assessment fills many a student with dread. Remember though — it's your chance to show what you can do. It won't be nearly as bad as you think it's going to be. Honest.

Be Imaginative

There are two tricky things about the speaking assessment — one is what to say, and two is how to say it. No matter how good your French is, it won't shine through if you can't think of anything to say.

Say you're asked to talk about your daily routine (or to imagine someone else's daily routine). It would be easy to give a list of things you do when you get in from school:

"Je fais mes devoirs. Je regarde la télé. Je mange. Je vais au lit."

= I do my homework. I watch television. I eat. I go to bed.

It makes sense, but the problem is, it's all a bit samey...

1) Try to think of when this isn't the case, and put it into an DIFFERENT TENSE:

"Mais demain je vais jouer au hockey après le collège."

= But tomorrow I'm going to play hockey after school.

2) Don't just talk about yourself. Talk about OTHER PEOPLE — even if you have to imagine them.

"J'ai regardé la télé avec mon frère, mais il n'aime pas les mêmes émissions que moi."

= I watched television with my brother, but he doesn't like the same programmes as me.

3) Give loads of OPINIONS and REASONS for your opinions.

"J'aime finir mes devoirs avant de manger. Puis je peux faire du sport plus tard."

= I like to finish my homework before eating. Then I can do sport later on.

A couple of 'DON'T's...

1) DON'T try to avoid a topic if you find it difficult — that'll mean you won't get any marks at all for that bit of the assessment. You'll be surprised what you can muster up if you stay calm and concentrate on what you do know how to say.
2) DON'T make up a word in the hope that it exists in French unless you're really, really stuck and you've tried all the other tricks on this page. If it's your last resort, it's worth a try.

Have Confidence

1) Believe it or not, the teacher isn't trying to catch you out. He or she wants you to do well, and to be dazzled by all the excellent French you've learned.
2) Speaking assessments can be pretty daunting. But remember it's the same for everyone.
3) Nothing horrendous is going to happen if you make a few slip-ups. Just try and focus on showing the teacher how much you've learnt.

Imagine there's no speaking assessment...

It's easy if you try. But that's not going to get you a GCSE. The main thing to remember is that it's much better to have too much to say than too little. Bear in mind the 3 ways to make your answers more imaginative. This will give you an opportunity to show off your beautiful French.

Hints for Speaking

Nothing in life ever goes completely according to plan. So it's a good idea to prepare yourself for a few hiccups in the speaking assessment. (Nothing to do with glasses of water.)

Try to find another way of saying it

There may be a particular word or phrase that trips you up. There's always a way round it though.

1) If you can't remember a French word, use an alternative word or try describing it instead.
2) E.g. if you need to say you want to be a doctor when you're older but you can't remember that 'doctor' is 'un médecin', then you could say 'Je veux travailler dans un hôpital' instead.
3) You can fib to avoid words you can't remember — if you can't remember the word for 'dog' then just say you've got a cat instead. Make sure what you're saying makes sense though — saying you've got a pet radio isn't going to get you any marks, trust me.
4) If you can't remember the word for a cup (la tasse) in your speaking assessment, you could say 'glass' (le verre) instead — you'll still make yourself understood.

If the worst comes to the worst, ask for help in French

1) If you can't think of a way around it, you can ask for help in the speaking assessment — as long you ask for it in French.
2) If you can't remember what a chair is, ask your examiner; "Comment dit-on 'chair' en français?" It's better than wasting time trying to think of the word.

You may just need to buy yourself some time

If you get a bit stuck for what to say, there's always a way out.

1) If you just need some thinking time in your speaking assessment or you want to check something, you can use these useful sentences to help you out:

Ben...	*Um...*	Pouvez-vous répéter, s'il vous plaît?	*Can you repeat, please?*
Eh bien...	*Well...*	Je ne comprends pas.	*I don't understand.*
Je ne suis pas sûr(e).	*I'm not sure.*	Ça, c'est une bonne question.	*That's a good question.*

2) Another good tactic if you're a bit stuck is to say what you've just said in a different way. This shows off your command of French, and also it might lead onto something else, e.g.:

"On mange en famille... Je ne mange pas seul, car mes parents rentrent à midi."

Saying the same thing a different way... leading on to another idea.

= We eat as a family... I don't eat on my own, because my parents come home at midday.

And don't be afraid to make mistakes — even native French speakers make 'em. Don't let a silly error shake your concentration for the rest of the assessment.

One last thing — don't panic...

Congratulations — you've made it to the end of the book. And without accident or injury, I hope — paper cuts hurt more than people think... Anyway, enough of this idle chit-chat. Read these pages, take on board the information, use it in your GCSE, do well and then celebrate in style.

A

à (à la, à l', au, aux) prep *at, to, in*
à mi-temps ad *part-time*
à peu près ad *about, roughly*
à travers ad *across*
l' abeille f *bee*
l' abricot m *apricot*
absolument ad *absolutely*
accepter v *to accept*
l' accès m *access*
accompagner v *to accompany*
l' accueil m *welcome, reception*
l' achat m *purchase*
acheter v *to buy*
l' acheteur m *buyer*
l' acier m *steel*
l' acteur/actrice m/f *actor/actress*
les actualités fpl *news, current affairs*
l' addition f *bill (restaurant)*
l' adolescent(e) m/f *adolescent, teenager*
adorer v *to adore*
l' adresse f *address*
s' adresser à vr *to apply to*
l' adulte m/f *adult*
l' aéroport m *airport*
les affaires fpl *business, items*
l' affiche f *poster, sign*
affreux/affreuse a *awful*
l' Afrique f *Africa*
l' âge m *age*
âgé(e) a *old, aged*
l' agence de voyages f *travel agency*
l' agenda m *diary*
l' agent de police m *policeman/woman*
l' agneau m *lamb*
agréable a *pleasant*
l' aide f *help*
aider v *to help*
l' ail m *garlic*
ailleurs ad *elsewhere*
aimable a *likeable, friendly*
aimer v *to like, love*
aîné(e) a *older (e.g. sister)*
ainsi ad *in this way*
l' air m *air, appearance*
en plein air ad *outdoors*
ajouter v *to add*
l' alcool m *alcohol*
l' Algérie f *Algeria*
(l') algérien(ne) a/m/f *Algerian*
l' alimentation f *food, groceries*
l' Allemagne f *Germany*
l' allemand m *German (language)*
(l') allemand(e) a/m/f *German*
aller v *to go*
aller à la pêche *to go fishing*
aller bien/mieux *to be well/better*
aller chercher *to fetch, pick up, meet*
s'en aller *to go away*
l' aller-retour m *return ticket*
l' aller simple m *single ticket*
allô interj *hello (when answering phone)*
s' allonger vr *to lie down*
allumer v *to switch on, light*
les Alpes fpl *Alps*
l' alpinisme m *mountaineering*
alors ad *then*
l' ambiance f *atmosphere*
améliorer v *to improve*
amener v *to bring*
amer, amère a *bitter*
(l') américain(e) a/m/f *American*
l' Amérique f *America*
l' ami(e) m/f *friend*
amical(e) a *friendly, amicable*
amicalement ad *in a friendly way*
l' amitié f *friendship*
amitiés *best wishes*
l' amour m *love*
amoureux/amoureuse a *in love*
amusant(e) a *amusing, fun*
amuser v *to amuse*
s'amuser vr *to enjoy oneself*
l' an m *year*
l' ananas m *pineapple*
ancien(ne) a *old, former*
l' anglais m *English (language)*
(l') anglais(e) a/m/f *English, English person*
l' Angleterre f *England*
l' animal domestique m *pet*
animé(e) a *lively, animated*
l' anneau m *ring*
l' année f *year*
l'année prochaine f *next year*
l' anniversaire m *birthday*
l' annonce f *advertisement*
l' annuaire m *phone book*
annuler v *to cancel*
l' ANPE f *job centre*
anxieux, anxieuse a *anxious*
août m *August*
apercevoir v *to notice*
à l' appareil *on the telephone*
l' appareil-photo m *camera*
l' appartement m *flat, appartment*
l' appel m *call*
appeler v *to call*
s'appeler vr *to be called*
appelle-moi/appelez-moi *call me (informal/formal)*
l' appétit m *appetite*
apporter v *to bring*
apprendre v *to learn*
l' apprenti(e) m/f *apprentice*
l' apprentissage m *apprenticeship*
(s')approcher v (r) *to approach*
approprié(e) a *appropriate*
après ad, prep *after*
après-demain ad *the day after tomorrow*
l' après-midi m/f *afternoon*
l' arbitre m *referee*
l' arbre m *tree*
l' architecte m/f *architect*
l' argent m *money*
l' argent de poche m *pocket money*
l' armée f *army*
l' armoire f *wardrobe*
l' arrêt m *stop*
l' arrêt d'autobus m *bus stop*
arrêter v *to stop (something)*
s'arrêter vr *to stop*
à l' arrière ad *at the back*
l' arrivée f *arrival*
arriver v *to arrive, to happen*
l' art dramatique m *drama*
les articles de sport mpl *sports equipment*
l' ascenseur m *lift*
l' aspirine f *aspirin*
s' asseoir vr *to sit down*
assez ad *quite, enough*
l' assiette f *plate*
l' assiette anglaise f *plate of cold meats*
l' atelier m *workshop*
l' athlétisme m *athletics*
(l') atlantique a/m *Atlantic*
attendre v *to wait*
en attendant *while waiting*
l' attention f *attention*
à l'attention de *for the attention of*
faire attention v *to be careful*
atterrir v *to land*
au prep = à le - *see* à
au bord de ad *alongside*
au bout de ad *at the end of*
au dehors de ad *outside of*
au dessous de ad *below*
au dessus de ad *above*
au fond de ad *at the bottom of*
au lieu de ad *instead of*
au milieu de ad *in the middle of*
au moins ad *at least*
au revoir interj *goodbye*
au secours! interj *help!*
l' auberge f *inn*
l' auberge de jeunesse f *youth hostel*
aujourd'hui ad *today*
auparavant ad *before*
aussi ad *too, as well, as*
aussi bien que ad *as well as*
l' Australie f *Australia*
(l') australien(ne) a/m/f *Australian*
l' auteur m *author*
l' auto f *car*
l' autobus m *bus*
l' autocar m *coach*
l' automne m *autumn*
l' automobiliste m/f *driver*
l' autoroute f *motorway*
autour (de) prep *around*
autre a *other*
autrefois ad *formerly*
autrement ad *otherwise*
l' Autriche f *Austria*
(l') autrichien(ne) a/m/f *Austrian*
aux prep = à les - *see* à
en avance ad *early*
à l' avant ad *before, in front of*
l' avantage m *advantage*
avantageux/avantageuse a *good value*
avant-hier ad *the day before yesterday*
avec prep *with*
avec plaisir *gladly*
l' avenir m *future*
à l'avenir *in the future*
l' aventure f *adventure*
l' averse f *shower (of rain)*
aveugle a *blind*
l' avion m *plane*
l' avis m *opinion*
à mon avis *in my opinion*
avocat m *lawyer, avocado*
avoir v *to have*
avril m *April*

B

le baby-sitting m *babysitting*
faire du baby-sitting v *to babysit*
le bac(calauréat) m *baccalauréat (equivalent of A-levels)*
les bagages mpl *luggage*
la bague f *ring*
la baguette f *baguette, stick*
se baigner vr *to bathe*
la baignoire f *bath*
le bain m *bath*
le baiser m *kiss*
le bal m *ball (dancing)*
le balcon m *balcony, circle*
la balle f *ball*
le ballon m *ball (big, e.g. football)*
la banane f *banana*
le banc m *bench*
baincaire a *banking*
la bande f *group*
la bande dessinée f *comic strip*
la banlieue f *suburbs*
la banque f *bank*
le bar m *bar*
barbant(e) a *boring*
la barbe f *beard*
la barrière m *gate*
le bas m *stocking*
bas(se) a *low*
en bas ad *downstairs*
le basket m *basketball*
les baskets fpl *trainers*
le bateau m *boat*
le bateau-mouche m *tourist boat on the Seine*
le bâtiment m *building*
la batterie f *drum kit*
battre v *to beat*
bavard(e) a *talkative*
bavarder v *to gossip*
beau/belle a *beautiful*
il fait beau *it's nice weather*
beaucoup (de) ad *lots (of), many*
le beau-fils m *son-in-law, stepson*
le beau-frère m *brother-in-law, stepbrother*
le beau-père m *father-in-law, stepfather*
le bébé m *baby*
(le/la) belge a/m/f *Belgian*
la Belgique f *Belgium*
la belle-fille f *daughter-in-law, stepdaughter*
la belle-mère f *mother-in-law, stepmother*
la belle-sœur f *sister-in-law, stepsister*
le besoin m *need*
avoir besoin de v *to need*
bête a *stupid*
la bêtise f *mistake*
le béton m *concrete*
le beurre m *butter*
la bibliothèque f *library*
le bic m *biro*
la bicyclette f *bicycle*
bien ad *well*
bien cuit(e) a *well done (meat)*
bien entendu interj *of course*
bien payé(e) a *well paid*
bien sûr ad *of course*
bientôt ad *soon*
à bientôt interj *see you soon*
la bienvenue f *welcome*
la bière f *beer*
le bifteck m *steak*
le bijou m *jewel, gem*
la bijouterie f *jewellery*
le/la bijoutier/bijoutière m/f *jeweller*
le billet m *ticket, banknote*
la biologie f *biology*
le bip sonore m *tone*
le bistro(t) m *café*
bizarre a *strange*
blanc(he) a *white*
blessé(e) a *wounded*
bleu(e) a *blue*
le bloc sanitaire m *showers, toilet block*
blond(e) a *blond(e)*
le blouson m *jacket*
la BNP f *Banque Nationale de Paris*
le bœuf m *beef*
bof! interj *huh! (shrug)*
boire v *to drink*
le bois m *wood*
la boisson (gazeuse) f *drink (fizzy)*
la boîte f *tin, can, box*
la boîte en carton f *cardboard box*
la boîte aux lettres f *postbox*
la boîte de nuit f *nightclub*
le bol m *bowl*
bon(ne) a *good*
bon anniversaire interj *happy birthday*
bon appétit interj *enjoy your meal*
bon marché(e) a *cheap*
bon voyage interj *have a good journey*
bon week-end interj *have a good weekend*
le bonbon m *sweet*
le bonheur m *happiness*
bonjour interj *good day, hello*
bon séjour interj *have a good stay*
bonne année interj *Happy New Year*
bonne chance interj *good luck*
bonne fête interj *have a good party*
bonne idée interj *good idea*
bonne nuit interj *good night*
bonnes vacances interj *enjoy your holiday*
bonsoir interj *good evening*
le bord m *edge*
au bord de la mer *by the sea*
la botte f *boot*
la bouche f *mouth*
le/la boucher/bouchère m/f *butcher*
la boucherie f *butcher's*
bouclé(e) a *curly*
la boucle d'oreille f *earring*
bouger v *to move*
le/la boulanger/boulangère m/f *baker*
la boulangerie f *baker's*
les boules fpl *bowls (ball game)*
le boulot m *work, job*
la boum f *party*
la bouteille f *bottle*
la boutique f *small shop*
le bouton m *button, spot*
le bowling m *bowling*
le bras m *arm*
bravo interj *bravo, well done*
bref/brève a *brief*
le bricolage m *DIY*
bricoler v *to do DIY*
le/la bricoleur/bricoleuse m/f *DIY-er*
briller v *to shine*
la brique f *brick*
briser v *to break*
(le/la) britannique a/m/f *British, British person*
la brochure f *booklet, brochure*
se bronzer vr *to sunbathe*
la brosse f *brush*
se brosser les cheveux vr *to brush one's hair*
le brouillard m *fog*
faire du brouillard v *to be foggy*
le bruit m *noise*
la brume f *mist*
brun(e) a *brown*
bruyant(e) a *noisy, loud*
le buffet m *sideboard, buffet*
le bulletin m *school report*
le bureau m *office, desk*
le bureau d'accueil m *tourist information office*
le bureau de change m *bureau de change, currency exchange*
le bureau de renseignements m *information service*
le bureau des objets trouvés m *lost property office*
le but m *goal, intention*

C

ça pron *that*
ça dépend *that depends*
ça fait combien? *how much does that come to?*
ça m'énerve *that annoys me*
ça me plaît (beaucoup) *I like it (very much)*
ça s'écrit comment? *how do you spell that?*
ça suffit *that's enough*
ça va(?) *I'm okay / how are you?*
ça ne va pas *I'm not well*
la cabine téléphonique f *phone box*
le cadeau m *present*
cadet(te) a *younger (e.g. sister)*
le café m *coffee, café*
la cafetière f *coffee pot*
le cahier m *notebook, exercise book*
la caisse f *counter, checkout*
le/la caissier/caissière m/f *cashier*
le calcul m *calculation, arithmetics*
la calculatrice f *calculator*
la calculette f *calculator*
calme a *calm*
le/la camarade m/f *friend, mate*
le camion m *lorry*
la camionnette f *van*
la campagne f *countryside, campaign*
le camping m *campsite*
le Canada m *Canada*
(le/la) canadien(ne) a/m/f *Canadian*
le canapé m *sofa, open sandwich*
le canard m *duck*
le/la candidat(e) m/f *candidate*
la canne (à pêche) f *stick, fishing rod*
la cantine f *canteen, dining hall*
capitale m *capital*
car conj *because, since*
le car m *coach*
la caravane f *caravan*
le carnet m *notebook, book of tickets*
la carotte f *carrot*
carré(e) a *square*
le carrefour m *crossroads*
la carrière f *career*
le cartable m *schoolbag, satchel*
la carte f *map, card, menu*
la carte bancaire f *bank card*

nouns — **m**: masculine **f**: feminine **pl**: plural **v**: verb **vr**: reflexive verb **a**: adjective

la carte de crédit f credit card
la carte d'identité f ID card
la carte postale f postcard
la carte routière f road map
le carton m cardboard
le cas m case
le casque m helmet
la casquette f baseball cap
cassé(e) a broken
le casse-croûte m snack, lunch
casse-pieds a pain in the neck
casser v to break
la casserole f saucepan
la cassette f cassette tape
le cassis m blackcurrant
la cathédrale f cathedral
à cause de conj because of
causer v to cause, to chat
la cave f cellar
le CD ROM m CD-ROM
le CDI (centre de documentation et d'information) m school library
la ceinture (de sécurité) f (seat) belt
cela pron that (i.e. that thing)
célèbre a famous
célibataire a single (not married)
(le)cent a/m hundred
le centimètre m centimetre
le centre m centre
le centre commercial m shopping centre
le centre de loisirs m leisure centre
le centre de recyclage m recycling centre
le centre de sport m sports centre
le centre sportif m sports centre
le centre-ville m city centre
cependant conj however
les céréales fpl cereal
la cerise f cherry
certainement ad certainly
le certificat m certificate
le CES = collège d'enseignement secondaire m secondary school
cesser v to stop
c'est-à-dire conj that's to say, meaning
c'est quelle date? phr what's the date?
la chaîne f TV channel, hi-fi system
la chaise f chair
la chaleur f heat
la chambre f bedroom
la chambre individuelle f single room
la chambre à deux lits f twin room
la chambre double f double room
la chambre de famille/familiale f family room
la chambre pour une personne f room for one person
le chameau m camel
le champ m field
le champignon m mushroom
le championnat m championship
la chance f luck
le changement m change
changer v to change
se changer vr to get changed
la chanson (populaire) f (pop) song
chanter v to sing
le/la chanteur/chanteuse m/f singer
le chapeau m hat
chaque a each
la charcuterie f delicatessen, pork butcher's
le/la charcutier/charcutière m/f pork butcher
charger v to load, charge
le chariot m trolley
le chat m cat
châtain(e) a chestnut coloured
le château m castle, palace
chaud(e) a warm, hot
le chauffage central m central heating
chauffer v to heat
le chauffeur (de taxi) m (taxi) driver, chauffeur
la chaussette f sock
la chaussure f shoe
chauve a bald
le/la chef m/f boss
le chemin m way, road, track, footpath
le chemin de fer m railway
le chemin de retour m the way back
la chemise f shirt
le chemisier m blouse
le chèque (de voyage) m (traveller's) cheque
cher/chère a, cher ad dear, expensive
chercher v to search for, to look for
le cheval m horse
les cheveux mpl hair
chez prep chez moi/toi at my/your house
chic a stylish
le chien m dog
le chiffre m number, figure
la chimie f chemistry
la Chine f China
(le/la) chinois(e) a/m/f Chinese
les chips mpl crisps
le chocolat m chocolate
le chocolat chaud m hot chocolate
le chœur m choir
choisir v to choose
le choix m choice
le chômage m unemployment
le chômeur m unemployed person
la chorale f choir
la chose f thing
le chou m cabbage
le chou-fleur m cauliflower
chouette a great
les choux de Bruxelles mpl Brussels sprouts
le cidre m cider
le ciel m sky
le cinéma m cinema
(le)cinq a/m five
(le)cinquante a/m fifty
cinquième a fifth
la circulation f traffic
le cirque m circus
les ciseaux mpl scissors
le citron m lemon
la civière f stretcher
clair(e) a light (colour), clear
la classe f class
classer v to file
le classeur m folder, ring-binder
le clavier m keyboard
la clé, clef f key
le clic m (mouse) click
le/la client(e) m/f customer
le climat m climate
cliquer v to click
le club des jeunes m youth club
le coca(-cola) m cola
le cochon d'Inde m guinea-pig
le code postal m postcode
le cœur m heart
le coffre m car boot
coiffé(e) de a wearing on head
le/la coiffeur/coiffeuse m/f hairdresser
la coiffure f hairstyle, headwear
le coin m corner
la colère f anger
en colère a angry
le colis m parcel
le collant m tights
la collection f collection
collectionner v to collect
le collège (technique) m secondary school (technical college)
le/la collègue m/f colleague
coller v to stick
le collier m necklace
la colline f hill
la colonie de vacances f holiday camp
combien ad how much, how many
le combiné m telephone receiver
la comédie f comedy
comique a funny
commander v to order
comme prep like
comme ci comme ça ad so-so
le commencement m start
commencer v to start
comment ad how
le commerce m business
le commissariat m police station
en communication avec a in communication with
le compartiment m compartment
complet/complète a full, complete
compliqué(e) a complicated
composer v to compose
composer le numéro v to dial the number
composter v to stamp (ticket)
comprendre v to understand
le comprimé m tablet (to swallow)
compris(e) a inclusive
y compris ad included
compter v to count
le comptoir m counter
le concert m concert
le/la concierge m/f caretaker
le concombre m cucumber
le concours m competition
les conditions de travail fpl working conditions
le/la conducteur/conductrice m/f driver
conduire v to drive
la conférence f conference, lecture
confiant(e) a confident
la confiserie f sweetshop
la confiture (d'oranges) f jam (marmalade)
le confort m comfort
confortable a comfortable
le congé m holiday
le congélateur m freezer
la connaissance f knowledge
connaître v to know (e.g. a person)
conseiller v to advise
la consigne (automatique) f left luggage (lockers)
contacter v to contact
content(e) a happy
contraire a contrary
contre prep against
le contrôle m test
le contrôle de passeports m passport control
contrôler v to control
le contrôleur m ticket inspector
le/la copain/copine m/f friend
copier v to copy
le corps m body
la correspondance f connection
le/la correspondant(e) m/f correspondent, penfriend
corriger v to correct
la côte f coast
le côté m side
à côté de prep next to
de chaque côté ad on both sides
d'un côté ad on one hand
de l'autre côté ad on the other hand, side
de tous côtés ad from each side
le coton m cotton
le cou m neck
couché(e) a lying down, in bed
se coucher vr to go to bed
la couchette f berth
la couette f duvet
la couleur f colour
de quelle couleur? what colour?
le couloir m corridor
le coup de main m helping hand
le coup de pied m kick
le coup de téléphone m phone call
couper v to cut
la cour f yard, playground
courir v to run
le courriel m e-mail
le courrier (électronique) m post (e-mail)
le cours m lesson
le cours de change m exchange rate
la course f running, race
les courses fpl shopping
faire les courses v to go shopping
court(e) a short
le coût m cost
le couteau m knife
coûter v to cost
la couture f sewing
couvert(e) a overcast (weather)
la couverture f blanket, cover
couvrir v to cover
la cravate f tie
le crayon m pencil
la crème f cream
la crème solaire f suncream
la crémerie f dairy (shop)
la crêpe f pancake
la crêperie f pancake restaurant
la crevaison f puncture
crevé(e) a burst, punctured
la crevette f prawn
le cri m call, shout
crier v to shout, scream
critiquer v to criticize
croire v to believe
le croissant m croissant
la croix f cross
le croque-monsieur m cheese and ham toastie
les crudités fpl raw salad items
la cuiller, cuillère f spoon
le cuir m leather
cuire (au four) v to cook (in the oven)
la cuisine f kitchen
le/la cuisinier/cuisinière m/f cook
la cuisinière f (à gaz / électrique) stove, cooker (gas / electric)
cuit(e) a cooked
le coup de téléphone m phone call
la culotte f shorts, knickers
cultiver v to cultivate, to grow
le curseur m cursor
le CV m CV
le cyclisme m cycling
le/la cycliste m/f cyclist

D

d'abord ad first (of all)
d'accord interj OK, I agree
d'habitude ad normally, usually
la dame f lady
le Danemark m Denmark
dangereux/dangereuse a dangerous
dans prep in, into
danser v to dance
la date de naissance f date of birth
de prep (du, de la, de l', des) of, from, some
de bonne heure ad early
de bonne humeur a in a good mood
de chaque côté ad from each side
de l'autre côté on the other side
de la part de qui? who from?, on whose behalf?
de rien don't mention it
de temps en temps ad from time to time
débarquer v to get off (e.g. boat)
débarrasser v to clear
debout a standing
se débrouiller vr to get on with it, to manage
le début m start, début
au début ad at the start
décembre m December
les déchets mpl rubbish
décider v to decide
décoller v to take off
découvrir v to discover
décrire v to describe
décrocher v to pick up (telephone)
déçu(e) a disappointed
dedans ad inside
défaire v to undo, unpack
défendre v to forbid, to defend
défense (f) de forbidden to
dégoûtant(e) a disgusting
le degré m degree
déguster v to taste
en dehors de prep outside of
déjà ad already
le déjeuner m lunch
le délai m waiting period, time limit
délicieux/délicieuse a delicious
demain ad tomorrow
à demain interj see you tomorrow
demander v to ask
démarrer v to start moving
déménager v to move house
le déménageur m removal man
demeurer v to live, to remain
demi(e) a half
le demi-frère m half-brother
la demi-pension f half-board
la demi-sœur f half-sister
démodé(e) a old-fashioned
la dent f tooth
le dentifrice m toothpaste
le/la dentiste m/f dentist
le départ m departure
le département m department (equivalent of county)
dépasser v to go past
se dépêcher vr to hurry
dépenser v to spend
déplacer v to move
le dépliant m leaflet
depuis prep since, for
dernier/dernière a last, previous
dernièrement ad lastly
derrière prep behind
désagréable a disagreeable
le désavantage m disadvantage
descendre v to go down
le désir m wish
désirer v to desire
désobéir v to disobey
désolé(e) a sorry
désordonné(e) a untidy
le dessin m art, drawing
le dessin animé m cartoon
dessiner v to draw
le dessinateur m designer
dessous ad below
dessus ad above
le détail m detail
se détendre vr to relax
détester v to hate
(le)deux a/m two
deuxième a second
devant prep in front of
devenir v to become
la déviation f diversion
devoir v to have to
les devoirs mpl homework
la différence f difference
différent(e) a different
difficile a difficult
la difficulté f difficulty
(le) dimanche m Sunday
la dinde f turkey
dîner v to dine
le dîner m supper, dinner
le diplôme m degree
dire v to say
le/la directeur/directrice m/f headteacher, manager
la disco(thèque) f disco
discuter v to discuss, to talk
disponible a available
disposer de v to have available
se disputer vr to argue
le disque compact m compact disc
la disquette f disc
les distractions fpl entertainment, things to do
distribuer v to distribute

divorcé(e) a *divorced*
(le)dix a/m *ten*
dixième a *tenth*
la dizaine f *about ten, ten or so*
le docteur m *doctor (male/female)*
le documentaire m *documentary*
le doigt m *finger*
le dommage m *damage*
quel dommage! interj *what a shame!*
donc ad *therefore*
donner v *to give*
donner à manger à v *to feed*
dont pron *of which, of whom*
dormir v *to sleep*
le dortoir m *dormitory*
le dos m *back*
le dossier m *file, folder*
la douane f *customs*
le/la douanier/douanière m/f *customs officer*
doubler v *to repeat a year, to overtake*
la douche f *shower*
se doucher vr *to shower*
la douleur f *pain*
douter v *to doubt*
Douvres *Dover*
doux, douce a *soft, mild (weather)*
la douzaine f *dozen*
(le) douze a/m *twelve*
le drap m *sheet*
le drapeau m *flag*
dresser v *to put up a tent, to train*
la drogue f *drug(s)*
se droguer vr *to take drugs*
droit(e) a *straight, right*
la droite f *right*
à droite a *on the right*
drôle a *funny*
dur(e) a/ad *hard, harsh*
durer v *to last*
dynamique a *dynamic*

E

l' eau f *water*
l'eau minérale f *mineral water*
l'eau potable / non potable f *drinking water / non-drinking water*
l' échange (scolaire) m *(school) exchange*
échanger v *to exchange, to swap*
s' échapper vr *to escape*
l' écharpe f *scarf*
les échecs mpl *chess*
l' éclair m *flash of lightening*
l' éclaircie f *sunny spell*
l' école f *school*
l'école primaire f *primary school*
l'école sécondaire f *secondary school*
les économies fpl *savings*
faire des économies v *to save money*
(l') écossais(e) a/m/f *Scottish, Scot*
l' Écosse f *Scotland*
écouter v *to listen*
je vous écoute *I'm listening*
l' écran m *screen*
s' écrier vr *to cry out, exclaim*
écrire v *to write*
l' écriture f *writing*
l' écrivain m *writer*
EDF f *French electricity company*
l' Édimbourg *Edinburgh*
l' éducation physique f *P.E.*
égal(e) a *equal*
ça/cela m'est égal *I don't mind*
également ad *equally*
l' église f *church*
égoïste a *selfish*

l' électricien(ne) m/f *electrician*
électrique a *electric*
électronique a *electrical, electronic*
l' élève m/f *pupil*
l' email m *e-mail*
embêtant(e) a *annoying*
embêter v *to annoy*
l' embouteillage m *traffic jam*
embrasser v *to kiss*
l' émission f *programme (e.g. TV)*
l'émission jeunesse f *children's programme*
l'émission musicale f *music programme*
l'émission sportive f *sports programme*
emmener v *to take (along)*
empêcher (de faire) v *to prevent (from doing)*
l' emplacement m *pitch (for tent)*
l' emploi m *job*
l' emploi du temps m *timetable, schedule*
l' employé(e) m/f *employee*
employer v *to employ*
l' employeur/employeuse m/f *employer*
emporter v *to take away*
emprunter v *to borrow*
le EMT m *CDT*
en prep *in, to, by (e.g. by plane), made of (e.g. of wool)*
enchanté(e) a *delighted (e.g. to meet someone)*
encore ad *still, yet, another*
encore de *more*
encore une fois ad *once more*
encourager v *to encourage*
endormi(e) a *asleep*
s' endormir vr *to go to sleep*
l' endroit m *place, area*
s' énerver vr *to get annoyed*
l' enfance f *childhood*
l' enfant (unique) m/f *(only) child*
enfin ad *at last*
enlever v *to remove*
l' ennui m *boredom, trouble*
s' ennuyer vr *to get bored*
ennuyeux/ennuyeuse a *boring, annoying*
énorme a *enormous*
enrhumé(e) a *having a cold*
l' enseignement m *teaching*
ensemble ad *together*
ensoleillé(e) a *sunny*
ensuite ad *next*
entendre v *to hear*
s'entendre vr *to get on*
s' entraîner vr *to train, to practise*
entre prep *between*
l' entrée f *entrance, admission, first course*
l'entrée libre f *free admission*
l' entreprise f *company*
entrer v *to go in*
l' entretien m *job interview, maintenance*
l' enveloppe f *envelope*
l' envie f *want, desire*
environ ad *around*
l' environnement m *environment*
les environs mpl *surroundings*
l' envoi de m *sending of, postage of*
envoyer v *to send*
envoyer un SMS v *to text*
épais(se) a *thick*
l' épaule f *shoulder*
épeler v *to spell*
l' épicerie f *grocery*
l' épicier/épicière m/f *grocer*
les épinards mpl *spinach*
épouser v *to marry*
l' époux/épouse m/f *spouse*
l' épreuve f *test*
l' EPS = éducation physique et sportive f *P.E.*
équilibré(e) a *balanced*
l' équipe f *team*
l' équipement m *equipment*

l' équitation f *riding (horses)*
l' erreur f *mistake*
l' escalade f *climbing*
l' escalier m *staircase*
l' escargot m *snail*
l' espace m *space*
l' Espagne f *Spain*
l' espagnol m *Spanish (language)*
(l') espagnol(e) a/m/f *Spanish, Spaniard*
l' espèce f *sort, kind, species*
espérer v *to hope*
l' espoir m *hope*
l' esprit m *spirit*
essayer (de) v *to try (to)*
l' essence f *petrol*
l' est m *east*
l' estomac m *stomach*
et conj *and*
l' étage m *storey, floor*
1er étage m *first floor*
2ème étage m *second floor*
l' étagère f *shelf*
l' état m *state*
les États-Unis mpl *United States*
l' été m *summer*
en été *in summer*
éteindre v *to turn off, put out*
l' étoile f *star*
étonné(e) a *surprised*
étonner v *to surprise*
étrange a *strange*
(à) l'étranger m *abroad*
être v *to be*
être bien chez v *to be at (checking correct number/address)*
être sur le point de v *to be about to*
l' être humain m *human being*
étroit(e) a *narrow*
l' étude f *study*
faire des études v *to study*
l' étudiant(e) m/f *student*
étudier v *to study*
l' euro m *Euro*
l' Europe f *Europe*
l' événement m *event*
évidemment ad *evidently, clearly*
l' évier m *sink*
exagérer v *to exaggerate*
l' examen m *exam*
l' excursion f *trip, excursion*
l'excursion scolaire f *school trip*
s' excuser vr *to apologise*
excusez-moi interj *I'm sorry, excuse me*
l' exemple m *example*
par exemple *for example*
s' exercer v *to train, practise*
l' exercice f *exercise*
l' expérience f *experiment*
expérimenté(e) a *experienced*
l' explication f *explanation*
expliquer v *to explain*
l' exposition f *exhibition*
exprès ad *on purpose*
(à l') extérieur a *outside*
extra a *fantastic*

F

fabriquer v *to make*
en face (de) prep *opposite*
fâché(e) a *angry*
se fâcher vr *to get angry*
facile a *easy*
la façon f *way*
le/la facteur/factrice m/f *postman/woman*
la facture f *bill, invoice*
faible a *weak*
la faim f *hunger*
faire v *to do, make*
faire le jardinage v *to do the gardening*
faire la lessive v *to do the laundry*

faire les magasins v *to go shopping*
faire le ménage v *to do the housework*
faire mal v *to hurt*
faire partie de v *to be part of*
faire du patin / du patinage v *to skate*
faire une pause v *to take a break*
faire la queue v *to queue*
faire un stage v *to do work experience*
faire les valises v *to pack*
le fait m *fact*
la famille f *family*
(le/la) fana(tique) a/m/f *fanatical, fan*
fana(tique) de a *fanatical about*
fantastique a *fantastic*
la farine f *flour*
fatigant(e) a *tiring*
la fatigue f *tiredness*
fatigué(e) a *tired*
la faute f *fault*
le fauteuil m *armchair*
faux/fausse a *false, wrong*
le faux numéro m *wrong number*
favorable a *favourable*
favori(e) a *favourite*
le fax m *fax*
les félicitations fpl *congratulations*
la femme f *woman*
la fenêtre f *window*
le fer m *iron*
la ferme f *farm*
fermé(e) a *closed*
fermé(e) à clef a *locked*
fermer v *to shut*
fermer à clef v *to lock*
la fermeture (annuelle) f *closing, closure (for holidays)*
le/la fermier/fermière m/f *farmer*
la fête f *party, feast, saint's day*
fêter v *to celebrate*
le feu m *fire*
le feu d'artifice m *firework*
le feu rouge m *red light*
les feux mpl *traffic lights*
la feuille (de papier) v *sheet (of paper)*
le feuilleton m *soap opera*
le feutre m *felt, felt-tip pen*
février m *February*
(le/la) fiancé(e) m/f/a *engaged, fiancé(e)*
la fiche f *sheet, form*
se fier v *to trust*
fier / fière a *proud*
la fièvre f *fever*
fièvreux/fièvreuse a *feverish*
la figure f *face*
le filet m *net*
la fille f *girl, daughter*
le film m *film*
film d'aventures m *adventure film*
film de guerre m *war film*
film d'horreur m *horror film*
film policier m *detective film*
film romantique m *romance film*
le fils m *son*
la fin f *end*
finir v *to finish*
les fléchettes fpl *darts*
la fleur f *flower*
le fleuriste m *florist*
le fleuve m *river*
flexible a *flexible*
le foie m *liver*
la foire f *fair, market*
la fois f *time*
à la fois a *at the same time*
foncé(e) a *dark*
le/la fonctionnaire m/f *civil servant*
fonctionner v *to function, to work*
le fond m *bottom*
au fond de prep *at the bottom, back of*
le foot(ball) m *football*
la forêt f *forest*
la formation f *training*

la forme f *shape*
être en bonne forme *to be fit*
formidable a *great*
le formulaire m *form*
fort(e) a *strong, loud*
fou/folle a *mad*
le foulard m *head scarf*
le four m *oven*
le four à micro-ondes m *microwave*
la fourchette f *fork*
la FR3 f *French TV channel*
frais/fraîche a *fresh*
la fraise f *strawberry*
la framboise f *raspberry*
le français m *French (language)*
(le/la) français(e) a/m/f *French, French person*
la France f *France*
franchement ad *frankly, honestly*
frapper v *to hit, strike*
le frein m *brake*
freiner v *to brake*
fréquemment ad *frequently*
fréquent(e) a *frequent*
fréquenter v *to go to*
le frère m *brother*
le frigo m *fridge*
frisé(e) a *curly (e.g. hair)*
les frites fpl *chips*
froid(e) a *cold*
le fromage m *cheese*
la frontière f *border*
le fruit m *fruit*
les fruits de mer mpl *seafood*
la fumée f *smoke*
fumer v *to smoke*
fumeur/non-fumeur a *smoking/non-smoking*

G

gagner v *to win, to earn*
le gallois m *Welsh (language)*
(le/la) gallois(e) a/m/f *Welsh, Welsh person*
le gant m *glove*
le garage m *garage*
le garagiste m *garage owner*
le garçon m *boy, waiter*
garder v *to keep*
la gare (SNCF) f *(railway) station*
la gare routière f *coach station*
la gare maritime f *port*
(se) garer v *to park*
le gasoil m *diesel*
le gâteau m *cake*
(la) gauche f/a *left*
à gauche a *on the left*
le gaz m *gas*
(la)GDF f *French gas company*
le gel m *frost*
la gelée f *frost*
geler v *to freeze*
le/la gendarme m/f *policeman/woman*
la gendarmerie f *police station*
général(e) a *general*
en général ad *generally, usually*
généralement ad *generally*
génial(e) a *great, of genius*
le genou m *knee*
le genre m *type, kind, sort*
les gens mpl *people*
gentil(le) a *nice, kind*
la géographie f *geography*
le/la gérant(e) m/f *manager*
le gîte m *self-catering cottage*
la glace f *ice cream*
le golf m *golf*
la gomme f *rubber*
la gorge f *throat*
le goût m *taste*
goûter v *to taste*
le gramme m *gram*
grand(e) a *big, great*
grand chose a *much*
le grand magasin m *department store*

la Grande-Bretagne f *Great Britain*
la grand-mère f *grandmother*
les grands-parents mpl *grandparents*
le grand-père m *grandfather*
gras(se) a *fatty*
gratuit(e) a *free (no cost)*
grave a *serious*
(le/la) grec/grècque a/m/f *Greek*
la Grèce f *Greece*
la grenouille f *frog*
la grillade f *grill*
griller v *to grill*
grimper v *to climb*
la grippe f *flu*
gris(e) a *grey*
gros(se) a *fat, big*
le groupe m *group*
la guêpe f *wasp*
le guichet m *ticket office*
la guitare f *guitar*
le gymnase m *gymnasium*
la gymnastique f *gymnastics*

H

habile a *skilful*
habillé(e) a *dressed*
l' habitant(e) m/f *inhabitant*
habiter v *to live in*
l' habitude f *habit*
habituel(le) a *usual*
s' habituer vr *to get used to*
le haricot m *bean*
haut(e) a *high*
en haut ad *upstairs*
la hauteur f *height*
hélas interj *alas*
l' herbe f *grass*
hésiter v *hesitate*
l' heure f *hour*
à l'heure ad *on time*
de bonne heure ad *early*
par heure ad *hourly*
quelle heure est-il? *what time is it?*
heurter v *to collide*
heureux/heureuse a *happy*
hier ad *yesterday*
l' histoire f *history, story*
l' histoire-géo f *history-geography*
historique a *historical*
l' hiver m *winter*
en hiver *in winter*
le/la HLM m/f = habitation à loyer modéré *council flat*
(le/la) hollandais(e) a/m/f *Dutch, Dutch person*
la Hollande f *Holland*
l' homme m *man*
honnête a *honest*
la honte f *shame*
l' hôpital m *hospital*
l' horaire m *timetable*
l' horloge f *clock*
le hors-d'œuvre m *starter*
l' hôtel m *hotel*
l' hôtel de ville m *town hall*
l' hôtesse d'accueil f *receptionist*
l' hôtesse de l'air f *air hostess*
l' huile f *oil*
(le)huit a/m *eight*
huitième a *eighth*
l' huître f *oyster*
l' humeur f *mood*
humide a *damp (weather)*
l' hypermarché m *hypermarket*

I

ici ad *here*
l' idée f *idea*
l' identité f *identity*
il faut *(we) must, it is necessary to*
il me faut *I need*
il me reste *I've got ... left*
il n'y a pas *there isn't/aren't*
il s'agit de *it's about*
il y a *there is, there are*
l' île f *island*
l' image f *picture*
immédiatement ad *immediately*
l' immeuble m *building, flats*
impatient(e) a *impatient*
l' imper(méable) m *raincoat*
impoli(e) a *impolite*
l' imprimante f *printer*
imprimer v *to print*
inclus(e) a *included*
l' inconnu(e) m/f *stranger, unknown (person)*
l' inconvénient m *disadvantage*
incroyable a *unbelievable*
l' Inde f *India*
(l')indien(ne) a/m/f *Indian*
l' indicatif m *area code*
indiquer v *to indicate*
individuel(le) a *individual*
l' industrie f *industry*
inférieur(e) a *lower*
l' infirmier/infirmière m/f *nurse*
l' informaticien(ne) m/f *computer scientist*
les informations (les infos) fpl *news*
l' informatique f *computer science*
informer v *to inform*
l' ingénieur m *engineer*
inquiet/-ète a *worried*
s' inquiéter vr *to worry*
l' instant m *moment*
pour l'instant *for the moment*
l' instituteur/institutrice m/f *primary school teacher*
l' instruction civique f *citizenship*
interdit(e) a *prohibited*
intéressant(e) a *interesting*
intéresser v *to interest*
s' intéresser à vr *to be interested in*
l' interêt m *interest*
(l') interieur a/f *inside, indoors, indoor*
l' internat m *boarding school*
l' interprète m *interpreter*
introduire v *to introduce*
inutile a *useless*
l' invitation f *invitation*
l' invité(e) m/f *guest*
inviter v *to invite*
l' irlandais(e) a/m/f *Irish, Irish person*
l' Irlande f *Ireland*
l' Irlande du Nord f *Northern Ireland*
l' Italie f *Italy*
(l')italien(ne) a/m/f *Italian*

J

j'en ai marre/assez *I've had enough, I'm fed up*
jaloux/jalouse a *jealous*
jamais — ne...jamais ad *never*
la jambe f *leg*
le jambon m *ham*
(le) janvier m *January*
le Japon m *Japan*
(le/la) japonais(e) a/m/f *Japanese, Japanese person*
le jardin m *garden*
le jardin publique m *public park*
le jardin zoologique m *zoological garden*
le jardinage m *gardening*
le/la jardinier/jardinière m/f *gardener*
jaune a *yellow*
le jean m *jeans*
jeter v *to throw (away)*
le jeu m *game*
le jeu de cartes m *card game*
le jeu de société m *board game*
le jeu électronique m *electronic game*
le jeu-vidéo m *video game*
(le)jeudi m *Thursday*
jeune a *young*
la jeunesse f *youth*
joli(e) a *pretty*
jouer v *to play*
le/la joueur/joueuse m/f *player*
le jouet m *game, toy*
le jour m *day*
c'est quel jour? *what day is it?*
le jour de congé m *day off (leave)*
le jour de l'An m *New Year's Day*
le jour férié m *public holiday*
le journal m *newspaper*
le/la journaliste m/f *journalist*
la journée f *day*
joyeux/joyeuse a *happy*
joyeux Noël interj *Merry Christmas*
le judo m *judo*
le juge m *judge*
juif/juive a *Jewish*
(le)juillet m *July*
(le)juin m *June*
le/la jumeau/jumelle m/f *twin*
jumelé(e) a *twin, twinned*
la jupe f *skirt*
le jus m *juice*
le jus de fruit m *fruit juice*
le jus d'orange m *orange juice*
jusqu'à prep *until, as far as*
juste a *just, fair*

K

le kilo m *kilo(gram)*
le kilomètre m *kilometre*
le kiosque à journaux m *newspaper stall*

L

là ad *there*
là-bas ad *over there*
là-haut ad *up there*
le laboratoire m *laboratory*
le lac m *lake*
laid(e) a *ugly*
la laine f *wool*
laisser v *to leave*
le lait m *milk*
la laitue f *lettuce*
la lampe f *lamp*
lancer v *to throw*
la langue f *language, tongue*
le lapin m *rabbit*
large a *wide, broad*
le lavabo m *washbasin*
le lave-vaisselle m *dishwasher*
laver v *to wash*
se laver vr *to wash oneself*
la leçon f *lesson*
le lecteur m *reader, player*
le lecteur DVD m *DVD player*
le lecteur MP3 m *MP3 player*
la lecture f *reading*
léger/légère a *light*
le légume m *vegetable*
le lendemain m *the next day*
le lendemain matin m *the following morning*
lent(e) a *slow*
lentement ad *slowly*
la lessive f *washing powder, washing*
la lettre f *letter*
lever v *to raise*
se lever *vr* *to get up*
la lèvre f *lip*
la librairie f *bookshop*
le/la libraire m/f *bookseller*
libre a *free*
libre-service a *free, self-service*
la licence f *university degree*
le lieu m *place*
avoir lieu v *to take place*
le lieu de naissance m *place of birth*
la ligne f *line*
la limonade f *lemonade*
lire v *to read*
la liste f *list*
la liste des prix f *price list*
la liste des hôtels f *hotel list*
le lit m *bed*
le litre m *litre*
le livre m *book*
le livre de poche m *paperback*
la livre sterling f *pound sterling*
livrer v *to deliver*
la location f *rental, hire*
la location de voitures f *car rental*
le logement m *accommodation*
loin (de) prep *far (from)*
lointain(e) a *far away, distant*
le lendemain m *the next day*
le loisir m *leisure*
les loisirs mpl *free time, leisure activities*
Londres *London*
long(ue) a *long*
longtemps ad *for a long time*
la longueur f *length*
louer v *to hire*
lourd(e) a *heavy*
la lumière f *light*
(le) lundi m *Monday*
les lunettes fpl *glasses*
les lunettes de soleil fpl *sunglasses*
luxueux/luxueuse a *luxury*
le lycée m *secondary school (years 11-13)*
le lycée technique m *secondary school for vocational training*
le/la lycéen/lycéenne m/f *secondary school pupil*

M

M6 *French TV channel*
le machin m *thing, contraption*
la machine à coudre f *sewing machine*
la machine à laver f *washing machine*
le maçon m *builder*
Madame f *Mrs, madam*
Mademoiselle f *Miss*
le magasin m *shop*
magnifique a *magnificent*
(le)mai m *May*
maigre a *thin*
le maillot m *vest*
le maillot de bain m *swimming costume*
le maillot de sport m *sports shirt*
la main f *hand*
maintenant ad *now*
le maire m *mayor*
la mairie f *town hall*
mais conj *but*
la maison f *house*
la maison des jeunes (MJC — la maison des jeunes et de la culture) f *youth club*
la maison individuelle f *detatched house*
la maison jumelée f *semi-detatched house*
la maison de la presse f *newsagent's*
le mal m *pain, evil*
mal ad *badly*
plus mal ad *worse*
le plus mal ad *worst*
mal payé(e) a *badly paid*
(le/la) malade a/m/f *ill, ill person*
la maladie f *illness*
malgré prep *despite*
malheureusement ad *unfortunately*
malheureux/malheureuse a *unhappy, unlucky*
la maman f *mum*
la manche f *handle*
la Manche f *the Channel*
manger v *to eat*
la manière f *manner, way*
le manque m *lack*
manquer v *to miss*
le manteau m *coat*
le maquillage m *make-up*
le/la marchand(e) m/f *shopkeeper*
la marche f *step, stair*
le marché m *market*
marcher v *to walk, to work*
(le) mardi m *Tuesday*
le mari m *husband*
le mariage m *marriage*
marié(e) a *married*
se marier vr *to get married*
le marketing m *marketing*
le Maroc m *Morocco*
(le/la) marocain(e) a/m/f *Moroccan*
la marque f *brand, label*
marrant(e) a *funny*
marre...en avoir *to have had enough, to be fed up*
marron a *brown (eyes, hair)*
(le)mars m *March*
le Massif Central m *centre of France*
le match m *match (sport)*
le match nul m *draw*
les maths fpl *maths*
la matière f *subject*
la matière facultative f *optional subject*
la matière obligatoire f *compulsory subject*
le matin m *morning*
la matinée f *morning*
mauvais(e) a *bad*
il fait mauvais *the weather's bad*
le/la mécanicien(ne) m/f *mechanic*
méchant(e) a *nasty*
le médecin m *doctor*
le médicament m *medicine*
la Méditerranée f *Mediterranean Sea*
meilleur(e) a *better*
le/la meilleur(e) a *the best*
meilleurs vœux *best wishes*
mélanger v *to mix*
le membre m *member, limb*
même a *same*
même ad *even*
même si conj *even if*
le ménage m *household, housework*
mener v *to lead*
mensuel(le) a *monthly*
le menu m *set menu*
menu à prix fixe m *fixed-price menu*
menu touristique m *tourist menu*
la mer f *sea*
merci interj *thank you*
(le) mercredi m *Wednesday*
la mère f *mother*
mériter v *to deserve*
merveilleux/merveilleuse a *marvellous*
le message m *message*
la messagerie vocale f *voice mail*
la mesure f *measure*
mesurer v *to measure*
le métal m *metal*
la météo f *weather forecast*
le métier m *job, profession*
le mètre m *metre*
le métro m *underground (tube)*
mettre v *to put*
mettre à la poste v *to post*
mettre la table v *to set the table*
se mettre en colère vr *to get angry*
se mettre en route vr *to take to the road*
le meuble m *piece of furniture*
meublé(e) a *furnished*
le midi m *midday*
le Midi m *South of France*
le miel m *honey*
mieux ad *better*
le mieux ad *the best*
mignon(ne) a *cute, sweet*
le milieu m *middle*
le/la militaire m/f *soldier*
mince a *slim*
le minuit m *midnight*
la minute f *minute*
dans une minute *in a minute*
le miroir m *mirror*
mixte a *mixed (e.g. school)*
la mobylette f *moped*
moche a *ugly, rotten*
la mode f *fashion*
moderne a *modern*
à moi a *mine*

ad: adverb **prep**: preposition **pron:** pronoun **interj**: interjection **conj**: conjunction

moins ad *less*
le moins ad *the least*
moins ... que *less ... than*
le mois m *month*
la moitié f *half*
le moment m *moment, time*
en ce moment ad *at the moment*
mon Dieu! interj *my God!*
le monde m *world*
le/la moniteur/monitrice (de ski) m *(ski) instructor*
la monnaie f *change (money)*
Monsieur m *Mr, sir*
la montagne f *mountain*
monter v *to rise*
la montre f *watch*
montrer v *to show*
la moquette f *fitted carpet*
le morceau m *piece*
la mort f *death*
mort(e) a *dead*
le mot m *word*
le mot de passe m *password*
le moteur m *motor*
la moto f *motorbike*
le/la motocycliste m/f *motorcyclist*
mouillé(e) a *wet*
la moule f *mussel*
mourir v *to die*
la moutarde f *mustard*
le mouton m *sheep*
le moyen m *means, way*
moyen(ne) a *medium*
le MP3 m *mp3*
municipal(e) a *public, municipal*
le mur m *wall*
mûr(e) a *mature*
le musée m *museum*
le/la musicien(ne) m/f *musician*
la musique f *music*
musique pop/rap/rock/classique f *pop/rap/rock/classical music*

N

nager v *to swim*
la naissance f *birth*
naître v *to be born*
la nappe f *tablecloth*
la natation f *swimming*
la nationalité f *nationality*
né(e) a *born*
né(e) le *born on*
ne ... jamais *never*
ne ... pas *not*
ne ... personne *no one*
ne ... plus *no longer*
ne ... que *only*
ne ... rien *nothing*
nécessaire a *necessary*
la neige f *snow*
neiger v *to snow*
nettoyer v *to clean*
nettoyer à sec v *to dry clean*
(le) neuf a/m *nine*
neuvième a *ninth*
neuf/neuve a *new*
le neveu m *nephew*
le nez m *nose*
ni… ni… conj *neither… nor...*
la nièce f *niece*
le niveau m *level*
(le)Noël m *Christmas*
noir(e) a *black*
le noix m *nut*
le nom m *name*
le nom de famille m *surname*
le nombre m *number*
nombreux, nombreuse a *many*
non interj *no*
non plus ad *neither, either (e.g. I haven't any either)*
le nord m *north*
normalement ad *normally*
la note f *mark, grade*
noter v *to note*
la nourriture f *food*
nouveau/nouvelle a *new*
de nouveau ad *again*
les nouvelles fpl *news*
le Nouvel An m *New Year*
(le) novembre m *November*
le nuage m *cloud*
nuageux/nuageuse a *cloudy*
la nuit f *night*
nul(le) a *useless*
le numéro m *number*
le numéro de téléphone m *telephone number*

O

obéir v *to obey*
l' obésité f *obesity*
l' objet m *object*
obligatoire a *compulsory*
obliger v *to oblige*
l' occasion f *opportunity (to)*
occupé(e) a *engaged, busy*
s' occuper de vr *to look after*
(l') octobre m *October*
l' odeur f *smell, fragrance*
l' œil m (pl. les yeux) *eye*
l' œuf m *egg*
l'œuf à la coque m *boiled egg*
l'œuf sur le plat m *fried egg*
les œufs brouillés mpl *scrambled eggs*
l' office de tourisme m *tourist office*
offrir v *to offer (a gift)*
l' oignon m *onion*
l' oiseau m *bird*
l' ombre m *shade, shadow*
l' omelette f *omelette*
on pron *one, you*
l' oncle m *uncle*
le onze a/m *eleven*
l' opinion f *opinion*
optimiste a *optimistic*
l' option f *option*
l' or m *gold*
l' orage m *storm*
orageux/orageuse a *stormy*
(l') orange a/f *orange*
l' orchestre m *orchestra*
ordinaire a *ordinary*
l' ordinateur m *computer*
l' ordonnance f *prescription*
ordonner v *to order*
l' oreille f *ear*
organiser v *to organise*
ou conj *or*
où ad *where*
où ca? *where's that?*
où est...? *where is...?*
oublier v *to forget*
l' ouest m *west*
oui interj *yes*
l' ours m *bear*
l' outil m *tool*
ouvert(e) a *open*
l' ouverture f *opening*
l' ouvrier/ouvrière m/f *worker*
ouvrir v *to open*

P

le paiement m *payment*
le pain m *bread*
le pain grillé m *toast*
la paire f *pair*
paisible a *quiet, peaceful*
la paix f *peace*
le palais m *palace*
pâle a *pale*
la pamplemousse f *grapefruit*
le panier m *basket*
en panne ad *broken down*
tomber en panne v *to break down*
le panneau m *sign, notice*
le pantalon m *trousers*
le papa m *dad*
la papeterie f *stationer's*
le papier m *paper*
le papier peint m *wallpaper*
(les) Pâques fpl *Easter*
le paquet m *parcel, packet*
par prep *by, per*
par chance ad *luckily*
par contre ad *on the other hand*
par hasard ad *on the off-chance*
paraître v *to appear*
le parapluie m *umbrella*
le parc m *park*
le parc d'attractions m *amusement park*
parce que conj *because*
le pardessus m *overcoat*
pardon interj *excuse me*
pardonner v *to forgive*
les parents mpl *parents*
paresseux/paresseuse a *lazy*
parfait(e) a *perfect*
parfois ad *sometimes*
le parfum m *flavour, perfume*
la parfumerie f *perfume shop*
le parking (souterrain) m *(underground) car park*
le parking à étages m *multi-storey car park*
parler v *to talk*
parmi prep *among*
la parole f *word, speech*
à part *on one side, separately, except for*
partager v *to share*
le/la partenaire m/f *partner*
particulier/particulière a *particular*
la partie f *part*
partir v *to depart, leave*
à partir de prep *from*
partout ad *everywhere*
pas — ne…pas ad *(...) not*
pas du tout ad *not at all*
pas encore ad *not yet*
pas mal de ad *quite a few*
le passage à niveau m *level crossing*
le/la passager/passagère m/f *passenger*
le/la passant(e) m/f *passer-by*
le passé m *past*
le passeport m *passport*
passer v *to pass*
je vous le passe *I'll put you through*
passer l'aspirateur *to vacuum*
passer un examen *to take an exam*
passer le temps à *to spend time doing*
se passer vr *to happen*
le passe-temps m *hobby*
passionnant(e) a *exciting*
le pâté m *pâté*
les pâtes fpl *pasta*
les patins à roulettes mpl *roller skates*
le patin(age) m *skating*
le patin(age) à glace m *ice skating*
le patin(age) à roulettes m *roller skating*
patiner v *to skate*
la patinoire f *ice rink*
la pâtisserie f *cake/pastry shop*
le/la pâtissier/pâtissière m/f *pastry chef, confectioner*
le/la patron(ne) m/f *boss*
la patte f *paw*
la pause f *break, pause*
la pause-café f *coffee break*
la pause de midi f *lunch break*
la pause-déjeuner f *lunch break*
la pause-thé f *tea break*
pauvre a *poor*
payer v *to pay*
le pays m *country*
le paysage m *countryside*
les Pays-Bas mpl *Netherlands*
le pays de Galles m *Wales*
le pays natal m *native country*
le péage m *toll*
la peau f *skin*
la pêche f *fishing, peach*
la peigne f *comb*
se peigner vr *to comb one's hair*
peindre v *to paint*
la peine f *sadness, difficulty*
la peinture f *painting*
la pelouse f *lawn*
pendant prep (conj) (+ que) *during, while*
la pendule f *clock*
pénible a *hard, tiring*
penser v *to think*
la pension complète f *full board*
perdre v *to lose*
perdu(e) a *lost*
le père m *father*
la permanence f *duty office*
permettre v *to allow*
le permis (de conduire) m *permit, (driving) licence*
la perruche f *budgerigar*
le personnage m *character*
la personnalité f *personality*
la personne f *person*
la perte f *loss*
peser v *to weigh*
pessimiste a *pessimistic*
petit(e) a *small, short*
le/la petit(e)-ami(e) m/f *boyfriend/girlfriend*
le petit déjeuner m *breakfast*
le petit-enfant m *grandchild*
le petit-fils m *grandson*
la petite-fille f *granddaughter*
le petit pain m *bread roll*
les petits pois mpl *peas*
le pétrole m *oil, petroleum*
peu ad *little, few*
peu cher a *cheap*
le peuple m *people*
la peur f *fear*
avoir peur *to be scared*
peut-être ad *perhaps*
le phare m *lighthouse, headlight*
la pharmacie f *pharmacy*
le/la pharmacien(ne) m/f *pharmacist*
la photo(graphie) f *photo(graph)*
la photocopie f *photocopy*
le/la photographe m/f *photographer*
la phrase f *sentence*
la physique f *physics*
le piano m *piano*
la pièce f *piece, coin, room*
la pièce de théâtre *play*
la pièce d'indentité f *proof of identity*
le pied m *foot*
à pied ad *by foot*
la pierre f *stone*
(le/la) piéton(ne) m/f/a *pedestrian*
la pile f *battery*
la pilule f *pill*
le pique-nique m *picnic*
pire a *worse*
le pire a *the worst*
la piscine f *swimming pool*
la piste f *track, trail*
pittoresque a *picturesque, vivid*
le placard m *cupboard*
la place f *square, room, space, seat*
le plafond m *ceiling*
la plage f *beach*
plaire (+ à) v *to please*
le plaisir m *pleasure*
le plan m *plan, map*
le plan de la ville m *map of the town*
la planche f *board*
la planche à roulettes f *skateboard*
la planche à voile f *windsurfing*
le plancher m *floor*
la plante f *plant*
le plastique m *plastic*
plat(e) a *flat*
le plat m *dish*
le plat du jour m *dish of the day*
le plat principal m *main course*
les plats cuisinés mpl *ready-made meals*
le plateau m *tray*
plein(e) a *full*
le plein air m *open air*
plein(e) de a *full of*
faire le plein v *to fill the car up*
plein(e) de vie a *full of life*
pleurer v *to cry*
pleuvoir v *to rain*
il pleut (à verse) *it's raining (pouring with rain)*
le plomb m *lead*
le plombier m *plumber*
la plongée sous-marine f *diving*
la pluie f *rain*
la plupart f *majority*
plus ad *more*
le plus ad *the most*
plus tard ad *later*
à plus tard interj *see you later*
plus ... que *more ... than*
plusieurs pron *several*
plutôt ad *rather*
pluvieux/pluvieuse a *rainy*
le pneu m *tyre*
la poche f *pocket*
la poêle f *frying pan*
le poids (lourd) m *(heavy) weight, lorry, HGV*
le poing m *fist*
à point a *medium (cooked)*
la pointure f *size (of shoe)*
la poire f *pear*
le poisson m *fish*
le poisson rouge m *goldfish*
le/la poissonier/poissonière m/f *fishmonger*
la poitrine f *chest*
le poivre m *pepper*
poli(e) a *polite*
la police f *police*
la police-secours f *emergency services*
le/la policier/policière m/f *policeman/woman*
pollué(e) a *polluted*
la pollution f *pollution*
la Pologne f *Poland*
(le/la) polonais(e) a/m/f *Polish, Polish person*
la pomme f *apple*
la pomme de terre f *potato*
le pompier m *fireman*
le pont m *bridge*
populaire a *popular*
le porc m *pork / pig*
le port m *harbour, port*
le portable m *mobile phone*
la porte f *door*
le porte clefs m *key ring*
la porte d'entrée f *front door*
le portefeuille m *wallet*
le porte-monnaie m *purse*
porter v *to carry, wear*
(le/la) portugais(e) a/m/f *Portuguese, Portuguese person*
le Portugal m *Portugal*
poser v *to pose, to place*
poser des questions v *to ask questions*
poser sa candidature v *to apply (for a position)*
positif/positive a *positive*
posséder v *to own, possess*
la poste f *post office*
le pot m *jar, pot, carton*
potable/non-potable a *drinkable/undrinkable*
le potage m *soup, broth*
la poubelle f *dustbin*
la poule f *hen*
le poulet m *chicken*
la poupée f *doll*
pour prep *for*
le pourboire m *tip*
pourpre a *purple*
pourquoi ad *why*
pourtant ad *yet*
pousser v *to push*
pousser un cri v *to cry out*
pouvoir v *to be able to*
pratique a *practical*
pratiquer un sport v *to do sport*
précieux/précieuse a *precious*
précis/précise a *precise*
préféré(e) a *favourite*
la préférence f *preference*

préférer v to prefer
premier/première a first
au premier étage on the first floor
en premier ad first of all
prendre v to take
le prénom m first name
préparer v to prepare
près (+ de) ad (prep) near, close
présenter v to present
presque ad almost
pressé(e) a busy
la pression f pressure
prêt(e) a ready
prêter v to lend
prévenir v to warn
les prévisions météo fpl weather forecast
prévu(e) a expected
prière de please (request)
principal(e) a main
principalement ad mainly
le printemps m spring (season)
la priorité à droite f give way to the right
privé(e) a private
le prix m price
le prix fixe m fixed price (e.g. menu)
le problème m problem
prochain(e) a next
proche a near, close
produire v to produce
le produit m product
le professeur m teacher
profond(e) a deep
la profondeur f depth
le programmeur m programmer
le progrès m progress
le projet m project
la promenade f walk
faire une promenade v to go for a walk
promener v to walk (i.e. a dog)
se promener vr to go for a walk
promettre v to promise
la promotion f promotion
propre a clean, own (e.g. my own room)
le/la propriétaire m/f owner
les provisions fpl groceries
la prune f plum
la publicité f publicity, advertisement(s)
puis ad then, next
puisque conj since
le pull(over) m jumper
punir v to punish
la purée f mashed potato
le pyjama m pyjamas
les Pyrénées m Pyrenees

Q

le quai m platform
la qualité f quality
quand conj/ad when
quand même all the same
quant à prep as for
la quantité f quantity
(le) quarante a/m forty
le quart m quarter
le quartier m district, part of town
(le) quatorze a/m fourteen
(le) quatre a/m four
(le) quatre-vingts a/m eighty
(le) quatre-vingt-dix a/m ninety
quatrième a fourth
que pron that, than
quel, quelle, quels, quelles pron which
quelque(s) a some
quelque chose pron something
quelque part pron somewhere
quelqu'un pron someone
quelquefois ad sometimes
qu'est-ce que / qu'est-ce qui pron what (in questions)
qu'est-ce que c'est? what is it?
qu'est-ce qu'il y a? what is there, what is it?
la question f question
la queue f tail, queue
que veut dire ... en anglais? what does ... mean in English?
qui pron who, that
la quinzaine f fortnight
(le)quinze a/m fifteen
(les) quinze jours mpl fortnight
quitter v to leave (e.g. a place)
ne quittez pas stay on the line
quoi pron what

R

raccrocher v to hang up (e.g. phone)
raconter v to tell
la radiomessagerie f paging
raide a straight
le raisin m grape
le raisin sec m raisin
la raison f reason
avoir raison v to be right
raisonnable a reasonable
ramasser v to pick up
la randonnée f hike
le/la randonneur/randonneuse m/f hiker
ranger v to tidy (e.g. a bedroom)
(le)rapide a/m quick, express train
rappeler v to call back
se rappeler vr to recall, to remember
le rapport m report, connection
les rapports mpl relationships
rarement ad rarely
se raser vr to shave
le rasoir m razor
rater v to miss
ravi(e) a delighted
rayé(e) a striped
le rayon m shelf, department (of a department store)
récemment ad recently
récent(e) a recent
la réception f reception
la recette f recipe
recevoir v to receive
recherché(e) a sought after
rechercher v to research
recommander v to recommend
reconnaissant(e) a grateful
la récréation f leisure, recreation, break(time)
le reçu m receipt
recycler v to recycle
la réduction f reduction
réduire v to reduce
réduit(e) a reduced
réel(le) a real
regarder v to look at
le régime m diet
la région f region
la règle f rule, ruler
le règlement m ruling, guideline
régler v to settle (bill)
regretter v to be sorry
régulier/régulière a regular
se relaxer vr to relax
religieux/religieuse a religious
remarquer v to notice
rembourser v to reimburse, to give back
remercier v to thank
remettre v to put back
remplacer v to replace
remplir v to fill (in)
la rencontre f meeting
rencontrer v to meet
se rencontrer vr to meet up
le rendez-vous m meeting
rendre v to give back
rendre visite à v to visit (a person)
renseigner v to inform
les renseignements mpl information
la rentrée f start of school year
rentrer v to return
la réparation f repair
réparer v to repair
le repas m meal
répéter v to repeat
le répondeur m answerphone
répondre v to reply
la réponse f reply
se reposer vr to rest
reprendre v to start again
le/la représentant(e) m/f representative
le RER (Réseau Express Régional) m regional train network
la réservation f reservation
réserver v to reserve
respecter v to respect, to observe
la responsabilité f responsibility
responsable a responsible
ressembler à v to look like, resemble
le restaurant m restaurant
rester v to stay
le résultat m result
le retard m delay
en retard ad late
le retour m return (journey)
retourner v (à) to return (to)
se retrouver vr to meet
la réunion f gathering
réussir v to succeed
le réveil m alarm clock
se réveiller vr to wake up
revenir v to come back
je reviens tout de suite I'll be right back
au revoir interj goodbye
la revue f magazine
le rez-de-chaussée m ground floor
le Rhin m Rhine
le Rhône m Rhone
le rhum m rum
le rhume m cold
riche a rich
le rideau m curtain
ridicule a ridiculous
rien pron nothing
ça ne fait rien it doesn't matter
rigolo(te) a funny
rire v to laugh
le risque m risk
la rivière f river
le riz m rice
la robe f dress
la robe de chambre f dressing gown
le robinet m tap
le rock m rock (music)
le roller m rollerblade, rollerblading
le roman m novel
le roman policier m detective novel
le roman-photo m graphic novel, comic
rond(e) a round
le rond-point m roundabout
rose a pink
rôti(e) a roast
rôtir v to roast
la roue f wheel
rouge a red
le rouge à lèvres m lipstick
rouler v to go (car)
la route f road
la route nationale f A-road
en route ad on the way
le routier m lorry driver
roux/rousse a red (hair)
le Royaume-Uni m United Kingdom
la rue f street
le rugby m rugby
(le/la) russe a/m/f Russian
la Russie f Russia

S

le sable m sand
le sac m bag
le sac à dos m rucksack
le sac à main m handbag
le sac de couchage m sleeping bag
le sac en plastique m plastic bag
sage a wise, good (child)
saignant(e) a bleeding, rare (meat)
sain(e) a healthy
la Saint-Valentin f Valentine's Day
saisir v to seize
la saison f season
la salade f salad, lettuce
la salade de pommes de terre f potato salad
le salaire m salary
sale a dirty
la salle f room
la salle à manger f dining room
la salle d'attente f waiting room
la salle de bains f bathroom
la salle de jeux f games room
la salle de séjour f living room
salut interj hi, bye
(le) samedi m Saturday
le SAMU (service d'aide médicale urgente) m mobile emergency medical service
la sandale f sandal
le sandwich m sandwich
sans prep without
sans doute ad without doubt
sans plomb ad unleaded
sans travail ad unemployed
la santé f health
en bonne santé a in good health
les sapeurs-pompiers mpl fire service
satisfaisant(e) a satisfying
satisfait(e) a satisfied
la saucisse f sausage
le saucisson m cold sausage
sauf prep except (for)
le saumon m salmon
sauter v to jump
sauvage a wild, undomesticated
sauver v to save
savoir v to know (e.g. how to do something)
le savon m soap
la science-fiction f science fiction
les sciences fpl science
(le/la) scientifique m/f/a scientific, scientist
scolaire a school
le SDF (sans domicile fixe) m homeless person
la séance f showing (e.g of film)
sec/sèche a dry
le sèche-cheveux m hairdryer
sécher v to dry
secondaire a secondary
la seconde f second
en seconde in year 11
le secours m help
au secours! interj help!
le/la secrétaire m/f secretary
la sécurité f security
(le)seize a/m sixteen
le séjour m stay
le sel m salt
selon prep according to
la semaine f week
semblable a similar
sembler v to seem
le sens de l'humour m sense of humour
à sens interdit ad no entry
à sens unique ad one-way
sensass a sensational
sensationnel(le) a sensational
sensible a sensitive
le sentier m path
le sentiment m feeling
sentir v to feel, smell
se sentir vr to feel
séparé(e) a separated
(le)sept a/m seven
septième a seventh
(le)septembre m September
la série (policière) f set, (police) series
sérieux/sérieuse a serious
le serpent m snake
serré(e) a tight
serrer v to grip, shake
le/la serveur/serveuse m/f waiter/waitress
serviable a helpful
la serviette f towel, napkin
le service m service
à votre service at your service
service (non) compris service (not) included
servir v to serve
se servir de vr to use
seul(e) a/ad only, alone
seulement ad only
sévère a strict
le shampooing m shampoo
le short m shorts
si conj if
s'il te plaît / s'il vous plaît ad please
le sida m AIDS
le siècle m century
le siège m seat
signer v to sign
silencieux, silencieuse a silent
simple a simple, single
le singe m monkey, ape
le sirop m syrup (medicine)
le site m site
situé(e) a situated
(le) six a/m six
sixième a sixth
en sixième in year 7
le skate m skateboarding
le ski m skiing
faire du ski v to go skiing
faire du ski nautique v to go water skiing
skier v to ski
le ski nautique m water skiing
le slip m knickers, underpants
la SNCF (Société nationale des chemins de fers français) f French national railway
la société f society, company
la sœur f sister
la soie f silk
la soif f thirst
le soir m evening
la soirée f evening
(le)soixante a/m sixty
(le)soixante-dix a/m seventy
le/la soldat(e) m/f soldier
les soldes mpl sales
le soleil m sun
sombre a dark
la somme f sum
le sommeil m sleep
le sommet m summit, top
le son m sound
le sondage m survey
sonner v to ring
la sonnette f doorbell
la sorte f sort, kind (of)
la sortie f exit
la sortie de secours f emergency exit
sortir v to go out
la sottise f stupidity
la soucoupe f saucer
soudain ad suddenly
souffrir v to suffer
souhaiter v to hope
la soupe f soup
sourire v to smile
la souris f mouse
sous prep under
le sous-sol m basement
sous-titré(e) a subtitled
le soutien-gorge m bra
se souvenir vr to remember
souvent ad often
les spaghettis mpl spaghetti
le sparadrap m sticking plaster
la spécialité (locale) f (local) speciality
le spectacle m show
le spectateur m spectator
splendide a splendid
le sport m sport
les sports d'hiver mpl winter sports
les sports nautiques mpl water sports
sportif/sportive a sporty
le stade m stadium
le stage (en entreprise) m work experience

ad: adverb **prep**: preposition **pron**: pronoun **interj**: interjection **conj**: conjunction

la station f *station, stop*
la station balnéaire f *seaside resort*
la station de métro f *underground station*
la station de ski f *ski resort*
la station de taxi f *taxi rank*
la station thermale f *spa town*
le stationnement m *parking*
stationner v *to park*
la station-service f *petrol station, service station*
le steward de l'air m *air steward*
stupide a *stupid*
le stylo m *pen*
le sucre m *sugar*
sucré(e) a *sweetened*
sucrer v *to add sugar*
les sucreries fpl *sweet things*
le sud m *south*
suffisamment ad *sufficiently, enough*
la Suisse f *Switzerland*
(le/la) suisse a/m/f *Swiss*
suite à prep *further to, following*
suivant(e) a *following, next*
suivre v *to follow*
le sujet m *subject*
super a *great*
superbe a *superb*
supérieur(e) a *superior, higher*
le supermarché m *supermarket*
le supplément m *extra, supplement*
supporter v *to put up with*
surprendre v *to surprise*
sur prep *on, on top of*
sur le point de *about to*
sûr(e) a *sure*
le surf m *surfing*
le surf des neiges m *snowboarding*
surfer sur internet v *to surf the internet*
la surprise f *surprise*
la surprise-partie f *surprise party*
le survêtement m *tracksuit*
surtout ad *especially*
SVP *(s'il vous plaît) please*
le sweat-shirt m *sweatshirt*
sympa(thique) a *nice, friendly*
le syndicat d'initiative m *tourist information office*

T

le tabac m *newsagent, tobacco*
la table f *table*
le tableau m *picture*
la taille f *size*
se taire vr *to be quiet*
tant ad *so much*
tant mieux *good, that's better*
tant pis *never mind, too bad*
la tante f *aunt*
taper v *to type, to knock*
le tapis m *carpet*
tard ad *late*
le tarif m *tarif, rate*
la tarte f *tart*
la tartine f *slice of bread and butter*
le tas m *pile, heap*
la tasse f *cup*
le taureau m *bull*
le technicien m *technician*
la technologie f *technology*
le téléphone m *telephone*
téléphoner v *to phone*
le téléviseur f *television set*
la télévision f *television*
le témoin m *witness*
la tempête f *storm*
le temps m *weather, time*
le temps libre m *free time*
de temps en temps ad *from time to time*
en même temps ad *at the same time*
tenir v *to hold*
le tennis m *tennis*
le tennis de table m *table tennis*
la tente f *tent*
en terminale *in upper 6th*
(se) terminer v(r) *to terminate, end*
le terrain m *ground*
le terrain de sport m *sports ground*
le terrain de camping m *campsite*
la terrasse f *terrace*
terrible a *terrible, dreadful*
la tête f *head*
le texte m *text*
le texto m *text message*
le TGV m *high-speed train*
le thé m *tea*
la théière f *teapot*
le théâtre m *theatre*
un tiers de m *a third of*
le timbre m *stamp*
timide a *shy*
tirer v *to pull*
le tissu f *material*
TlJ see tous les jours
les toilettes fpl *toilets*
le toit m *roof*
la tomate f *tomato*
tomber v *to fall*
tondre v *to cut, to mow*
le tonnerre m *thunder*
le tort m *fault, wrong*
avoir tort v *to be wrong*
la tortue f *tortoise*
tôt ad *early*
tôt ou tard *sooner or later*
la touche f *key, button, touch*
toucher v *to touch*
toujours ad *always*
la tour f *tower*
le tourisme m *tourism*
le/la touriste m/f *tourist*
touristique a *touristy*
tourner v *to turn*
tous m *everyone*
tous les deux a *both*
tous les jours ad *every day*
tousser v *to cough*
tout, toute, tous, toutes a/ad/pron *all*
tout à coup ad *all of a sudden*
tout à fait ad *quite, completely*
à toute à l'heure interj *see you later*
tout de suite ad *immediately*
tout droit ad *straight ahead*
tout le monde pron *everyone*
tout près m *close by*
toutes directions fpl *all directions (on road sign)*
toutes les cinq minutes *every five minutes*
la toux f *cough*
la traduction f *translation*
traduire v *to translate*
le train m *train*
être en train de faire quelque chose *to be in the process of doing something*
le traitement m *treatment*
traiter de v *to deal with*
le trajet m *journey*
le tramway m *tram*
la tranche f *slice*
tranquille a *quiet*
les transports en commun mpl *public transport*
le travail m (pl. les travaux) *work, roadworks*
les travaux manuels mpl *handicrafts*
travailler v *to work*
travailleur/travailleuse a *hard-working*
la traversée f *crossing*
traverser v *to cross (e.g. street)*
(le)treize a/m *thirteen*
tremper v *to soak*
(le)trente a/m *thirty*
très ad *very*
le tricot m *jumper*
tricoter v *to knit*
le trimestre m *term*
triste a *sad*
(le)trois a/m *three*
troisième a *third*
se tromper vr *to make a mistake*
la trompette f *trumpet*
trop ad *too, too much*
le trottoir m *pavement*
le trou m *hole*
la trousse f *small case, pencil case*
trouver v *to find*
se trouver vr *to be (situated)*
le truc m *thing, trick*
la truite f *trout*
le tube m *tube, hit song*
tuer v *to kill*
la Tunisie f *Tunisia*
(le/la) tunisien(ne) a/m/f *Tunisian*
le Tunnel (sous la Manche) m *the Channel Tunnel*
le tuyau m *pipe*
le TVA m *VAT*
le type m *bloke, type*
typique a *typical*

U

un/une/des art/a *a, one, some*
l' uniforme m *uniform*
l' UE (Union européenne) f *European Union*
unique a *only*
l' université f *university*
l' usine f *factory*
utile a *useful*
utiliser v *to use*

V

les vacances fpl *holiday, vacation*
le/la vacancier/vacancière m/f *holidaymaker*
la vache f *cow*
la vague f *wave*
la vaisselle f *washing-up*
faire la vaisselle v *to wash up*
valable a *valid*
la valeur f *value*
d'une grande valeur a *valuable*
la valise f *suitcase*
la vallée f *valley*
le vandalisme m *vandalism*
la vanille f *vanilla*
la vapeur f *steam*
varié(e) a *varied*
variable a *variable, unsettled*
il vaut (la peine) *it is worth (the trouble)*
le veau m *veal*
la vedette f *star (e.g. film star)*
(le/la) végétarien(ne) a/m/f *vegetarian*
le véhicule m *vehicle*
le vélo m *bike*
le vélomoteur m *moped*
le/la vendeur/vendeuse m/f *shop assistant*
vendre v *to sell*
(le) vendredi m *Friday*
venir v *to come*
le vent m *wind*
la vente f *sale*
le ventre m *stomach*
le verglas m *(black) ice*
vérifier v *to check, verify*
la vérité f *truth*
le verre m *glass*
vers prep *around, about, towards*
la version française f *film dubbed into French*
la version originale f *film in the original language, with subtitles*
vert(e) a *green*
la veste f *jacket*
le vestiare m *cloakroom*
le vestibule m *hall*
les vêtements mpl *clothes*
le/la vétérinaire m/f *vet*
vêtu(e) m *clothed*
la viande f *meat*
vide a *empty*
vider v *to empty*
la vie f *life*
le/la vieillard/vieillarde m/f *old person*
vif/vive a *lively*
vieux/vieille a *old*
vilain(e) a *ugly, naughty*
le village m *village*
la ville f *town*
en ville *in town*
le vin m *wine*
le vinaigre m *vinegar*
(le) vingt a/m *twenty*
la vingtaine f *about twenty, twenty or so*
violet(te) a *purple*
le violon m *violin*
le virage m *bend*
le visage m *face*
la visite (guidée) f *(guided) visit*
visiter v *to visit (a place)*
la vitamine f *vitamin*
vite ad *quickly*
la vitesse f *speed*
le vitre m *window, pane*
la vitrine f *window*
vivre v *to live*
le vocabulaire m *vocabulary*
le vœu m *wish*
voici interj *here is, here are*
voilà interj *there is, there are*
la voile f *sailing*
voir v *to see*
se voir vr *to see each other*
voisin(e) a *neighbouring*
le/la voisin(e) m/f *neighbour*
la voiture f *car*
la voix f *voice*
le vol m *flight, theft*
le volant m *steering wheel*
voler v *to fly, to steal*
le voleur m *thief*
le volley m *volleyball*
volontiers ad *gladly, willingly, with pleasure*
vomir v *to vomit*
vouloir v *to want*
vouloir dire v *to mean*
le voyage m *journey*
voyager v *to travel*
vrai(e) a *true*
vraiment ad *really*
le VTT (vélo tout-terrain) m *mountain bike*
la vue f *sight, view*
la vue de mer f *sea view*

W

le wagon-lit m *sleeping car*
le wagon-restaurant m *restaurant car*
les W.C. mpl *W.C.*
le web m *web*
le web-mail m *webmail*
le week-end m *weekend*

X,Y

y pron *there, to it etc.*
le yaourt m *yoghurt*
les yeux mpl *eyes (plural of l'oeil)*

Z

la zone f *zone*
la zone piétonne f *pedestrian zone*
le zoo m *zoo*

KEY

m:	masculine noun
f:	feminine noun
pl:	plural noun
v:	verb
vr:	reflexive verb
a:	adjective (describes a noun)
ad:	adverb (describes a verb/adjective)
prep:	preposition (connects the verb to a place, thing or person: e.g. 'to', 'for')
pron:	pronoun (replaces noun: e.g. 'he', 'me')
interj:	interjection (stands alone: e.g. 'Hello!')
conj:	conjunction (connects two parts of a sentence: e.g. 'and', 'because')
art:	article (e.g. 'the', 'a')

Index